Critical Guides to French Texts

Critical Guides to French Texts

EDITED BY ROGER LITTLE, WOLFGANG VAN EMDEN, DAVID WILLIAMS

JARRY

Ubu Roi

Keith Beaumont

Lecturer in French
University of Leicester

Grant & Cutler Ltd
1987

Library of Congress Cataloging-in-Publication Data

Beaumont, Keith, 1944-
  Jarry, Ubu roi.

  (Critical guides to French texts: 69)
  Bibliography: p.
  1. Jarry, Alfred, 1873-1907. Ubu roi. I. Title. II. Title: Ubu roi. III. Series.
PQ2619.A65U378 1987 842'.8 87-23709
ISBN 0-7293-0268-7 (pbk.)

I.S.B.N. 84-599-2168-9

DEPÓSITO LEGAL: V. 2.581 - 1987

Printed in Spain by
Artes Gráficas Soler, S.A., Valencia
for
GRANT & CUTLER LTD
55-57, GREAT MARLBOROUGH STREET, LONDON W1V 2AY
and
27, SOUTH MAIN STREET, WOLFEBORO, NH 03894-2069, USA

Contents

Contents

Prefatory Note

Page references for Jarry's writings on the theatre are to the 'Folio' edition of *Ubu*, edited by Noël Arnaud and Henri Bordillon, Gallimard, 1978, the best edition to date of the *Ubu* plays. Other references for Jarry's works are, unless otherwise indicated, to the *Œuvres complètes* edited by Michel Arrivé, Gallimard (Bibliothèque de la Pléiade), volume I, 1972, abbreviated to *O.C.*, I. References with italicized numbers (e.g. *18*, p.160) are to items in the bibliography at the end of the present study.

1. Introduction: The Enigma of Ubu

'Merdre!': the very first word of Jarry's *Ubu Roi*, spoken by the actor Firmin Gémier on that memorable evening in Paris on 10 December 1896, was the signal for one of the greatest scandals which the French theatre had ever seen. The delivery of that one word provoked such an uproar in the auditorium that it was some twenty minutes before the performance could resume, and it continued to be interrupted throughout by similar, if less pro-longed, outbursts of anger and indignation. The theatrical bombshell which Jarry had thus exploded was to leave an imprint on the theatre, both in France and elsewhere, which can rarely if ever have been equalled by any other single play. But however great the sense of moral outrage generated by that per-formance, the aesthetic revolution which it inaugurated is, from our point of view, far more significant. The how and why of that revolution is to be the chief subject of this study.

All successful revolutions end of course by becoming part of an established order, and *Ubu Roi* is no exception. Today the play has become an accepted part of the theatrical repertoire and figures widely on the syllabuses of courses in modern French, and indeed European, drama. And yet, for all its acceptance, performances of the play continue to display a bewildering diversity of approach and to provoke in audiences a gamut of reactions ranging from shock through bewilderment and incomprehension to uninhibited hilarity. This diversity of approach, and of reaction on the part of audiences, is such as to give rise to a series of questions concerning *Ubu Roi* which I have endeavoured to outline in the pages following.

The first of these questions concerns the very nature of the play. When confronted with the task of staging *Ubu Roi* its original producer, Aurélien Lugné-Poe, found himself in a state of total perplexity. As he himself later admitted in his memoirs speaking of the text of the play, 'je ne savais par quel bout [le] prendre pour le réaliser à la scène' (*20*, p.160). At one point, in fact, he had even wanted to produce the play as a tragedy! His perplexity has been paralleled by that of many subsequent directors (and indeed that of many readers) confronted with Jarry's text. Peter Brook put his finger nicely on the nature of the problem when he stated in an interview with Jean-Claude Carrière on the French television channel FR3 in 1977 that the text of the play was difficult to relate to since 'il n'y a pas de psychologie, il n'y a pas les références habituelles qui permettent de dire: ah oui, je sais comment pénétrer derrière ce texte'. At the most basic level, therefore, the question arises, what *kind* of play is this? Is it to be seen in terms of mere farce and slapstick? Or in terms of total 'absurdity'? Or as a form of satire? Or perhaps even, along with Lugné-Poe, as 'tragedy'?

A second question (or series of questions) arises from the reaction of the audience on the occasion of that first performance of 1896. Why precisely should it have reacted with such a sense of shock and outrage? And more significantly, from our point of view, *can* a performance of *Ubu Roi* produce the same reaction today? Indeed, *should* a modern director aim at producing a reaction of shock and scandal? Or is it the case that changed tastes and expectations on the part of theatre audiences make it necessary to aim for different reactions and to emphasize other aspects of the work than those which seemed most in evidence to the audience of 1896?

A third question concerns the fortunes of the play. How is it that *Ubu Roi*, after decades of near-neglect following its original *succès de scandale*, has since about 1950 been increasingly performed by amateur and professional companies alike? What is the role played in this by political and social factors, and how much does the popularity — or the notoriety — of the monstrous figure of Ubu owe to the historical experience of the last fifty or sixty years? Or, on a quite different plane, to what extent does the growing popularity of the play correspond to a change in our sensibility — to a growing awareness of what has come to be known as 'the absurd' and to a growing receptivity to what we might call 'absurd' humour?

Then there is the problem of the 'significance' of the figure of

Ubu himself. Ubu has been seen as everything from an embodiment of political 'anarchism' to a satire upon the 'bourgeois', or the prophetic embodiment of any number of totalitarian dictators of this century, or even, in Cyril Connolly's colourful (but meaningful?) phrase, 'the Santa Claus of the Atomic Age' (quoted in *25*, p.10). Indeed, as Jürgen Grimm aptly comments, 'scarcely any other figure in the modern theatre, with the possible exception of "Godot", has given rise to such a vast number of contradictory interpretations' (*18*, p.62). To what extent are such diverse interpretations justified? And what does their very diversity tell us about the nature of the play itself?

Lastly, there is the question of the relationship existing between Jarry's plays and conception of the theatre and developments since his death. Jarry is often cited in general terms as a precursor, and even a source of influence, in histories of the modern French theatre and in particular in studies of the so-called 'theatre of the absurd'. What really is the relationship between his work and that of later playwrights? Is *Ubu Roi* really concerned with the projection of a view of an 'absurd' universe, as has been so often alleged? Or does the play's real originality and importance lie in its being an experiment in a radically new conception of dramatic form and technique? These are questions to which I shall endeavour to provide an answer in the final chapter of this study.[1]

---

[1] It is not part of the purpose of this study to examine the relationship between *Ubu Roi* and the other *Ubu* plays (*Ubu cocu*, *Ubu enchaîné*, *Ubu sur la Butte*), nor the complex question of the relationship between these plays and the remainder of Jarry's rich and varied literary work. The same applies to such biographical questions as the supposed (but in reality quite erroneous) 'identification' between Jarry and his monstrous creation Ubu, and to the question of the relationship sometimes alleged to exist between Jarry's theatre and the principles of his 'science of pataphysics'. For a detailed discussion of these and other similar issues, see *9*.

2. Historical Background

It is now widely known that the original model for the figure of
Ubu was a physics teacher encountered by Jarry at the Lycée de
Rennes, in Brittany, which he entered in October 1888 at the age
of 15. The enormously fat, well-meaning but grotesquely incom-
petent figure of Félix Hébert had been terrorized and mocked by
countless generations of schoolboys, and had been for many
years before Jarry's arrival at the school — under the names
variously of 'le Père Heb', 'le Père Ebé' and 'le P.H.' — the
hero/villain of a series of schoolboy mock epics and extravagant
tales of adventure inspired by authors such as Rabelais, Lesage
and a host of others. Existing originally in oral form, a number
of these tales had been written down and elaborated upon by a
pupil named Charles Morin in the years immediately preceding
Jarry's arrival at the school. These literary efforts culminated in
a play entitled *Les Polonais* which recounted the murder by 'le
P.H.' of the King of Poland, Wenceslas, his seizure of the
throne, and his subsequent defeat at the hands of the Russian
Tsar and expulsion from Poland.

It was this text which, according to a polemical work
published in 1921 by a former pupil of the Lycée, Charles
Chassé, under the title of *Sous le masque d'Alfred Jarry(?). Les
Sources d'Ubu-Roi* [sic], was simply 'pirated' by Jarry and
eventually published with the title of *Ubu Roi*. The controversy
sparked off by Chassé's book — the second 'battle of *Ubu Roi*',
as it has been called — resounded throughout the press and
publishing world for months and even years after its publication. But though the book contains a mine of valuable
information about the origins of the play and of the figure of
Ubu, Chassé's thesis is both factually inaccurate and miscon-
ceived. It is not true that Jarry systematically tried to hide the
fact that he was not the play's sole or original author. Secondly,
his own contribution to the work was undoubtedly, even on

Chassé's own evidence, considerably greater than the latter alleged.[2] Lastly, and most fundamentally of all, neither *Ubu Roi* nor *Les Polonais*, nor Morin's other creations, could ever have come into existence without the vast and shapeless mass of schoolboy legend and fantasy out of which all were created. In the fullest possible sense — and this perhaps provides a key to much of its appeal — *Ubu Roi* is the fruit of a collective schoolboy imagination, an authentic product of a collective, 'primitive' creativity, in a far more real sense than much of what in our culture passes for 'popular' or 'folk' art.

Moreover, there are several important respects in which Jarry has an even greater claim to the play than Charles Morin. Where Morin was only too willing, upon entering the 'serious' world of adulthood, to leave behind (in his own words) this *bêtise* and *couillonnade* of childhood, it was Jarry, and he alone, who rescued it from oblivion. Secondly, it was Jarry alone — and this is disputed by no-one — who invented the *name* Ubu, a name which has had much to do with the play's subsequent fame. And, perhaps most significant of all, it was he and he alone who realized the potential of the play as *theatre*, and who set about almost from the first putting it on the stage.

The first of these performances were given by the pupils of the Lycée themselves on a makeshift live stage set up by Jarry and Henri Morin, Charles's younger brother. They were followed

---

[2] The question of Jarry's precise contribution to the elaboration of the text of *Ubu Roi* can now never be definitively answered (apart from the certain fact of his invention of the name Ubu), though it must have been substantial since, from Charles Morin's own account of his original version of *Les Polonais*, this cannot have been more than half the length of the final version of the play. It is worth noting however in this connection that there is a slight but significant difference in the character of Ubu and, as a result, in the texture of the writing in the last two acts of *Ubu Roi*. Ubu tends here to be a more loquacious character (bearing more resemblance in this respect to the hero of *Ubu cocu* and *Ubu enchaîné*, both of which are certainly Jarry's work), much given to making feeble or idiotic puns and jokes. (A similar loquaciousness is to be found also in Mère Ubu, who is responsible for by far the longest monologue in the play, in Act V, Scene 1.) The language is also less crude and violent, and there is a greater element of verbal invention (of the type *corne d'Ubu*, *ciseau à merdre*, etc.). And where Ubu in the early part of the play is characterized above all by blundering monstrosity and naïve stupidity, here it is the element of sheer silliness which is uppermost. These facts taken together suggest that it is perhaps in the last two acts of the play that Jarry's greatest contribution to the elaboration of *Ubu Roi* is to be found, although such a conclusion must remain hypothetical.

shortly afterwards by a series of performances in Jarry's and
Morin's newly created puppet theatre, or *guignol*, to which they
gave the name of 'Le Théâtre des Phynances'. The *guignol*, a
Punch-and-Judy type puppet theatre enormously popular with
audiences of children and adults alike throughout the nineteenth
century, had been an object of fascination for Jarry ever since
early childhood. And, significantly, it was these puppet performances, rather than the preceding experiment in live theatre,
that Jarry chose to remember when he later came to prepare *Ubu
Roi* for publication.

Although the language of the play will be examined in a later
chapter, it may be useful here to explain a number of terms and
motifs which form part of the original schoolboy folklore of the
Lycée de Rennes. The chief preoccupation of 'le Père Heb' was
the quest for *phynance* (plunder), which he loaded into an
enormous sack, his *poche* (or *pôche*). He was aided in this by his
faithful henchmen, the *palotins* (their full title was *palotins à
phynance*, a development from Charles Morin's *salopins à
finance* which still survives, alongside the new name, in *Ubu
Roi*). (These were in origin the pupils of the Lycée themselves, in
particular the boarders, as the song which they sing in Act I,
Scene 6 of *Ubu cocu* reveals.) The *palotins*' chief victims were
the *rentiers* (those who lived from investments, in particular
government bonds), inflicting unspeakable tortures upon all
who refused to pay up by means of three ingenious devices —
the *pal*, a kind of stake upon which their victims were impaled;
the *trappe* (synonymous with the *Chambre-à-Sous* and *Pince-
Porc*), which appears to have been a fusion of some hideous
underground torture-chamber and a cess-pit; and the *machine à
décerveler*, immortalized in the *Chanson du Décervelage* and
actually figuring in the cast list of the final edition of *Ubu Roi* in
1900. Two further, otherwise inexplicable, motifs are the *chiens
à bas de laine*, whose task was to divest the *rentiers* of their shoes
and stockings, and the *chandelle verte*, the subject of Ubu's oft-
repeated oath, which was originally simply a candle placed in his
window as a signal to his henchmen.

On leaving Rennes for Paris, Jarry, refusing to leave such
childhood 'stupidities' behind him, carried the manuscript of the

future *Ubu Roi* not only to the capital, but also into the very heart of the hallowed citadel of Symbolism. Here he continued to recite and to perform the play, together with *Ubu cocu*, on a makeshift puppet theatre which he set up. And he was soon, from 1894 onwards, giving readings of *Ubu Roi* at least to the Symbolist faithful assembled at the Tuesday evening gatherings of the *Mercure de France*. The play was finally published in 1896, to be followed by a second, facsimile edition a year later and a third and final edition, jointly with *Ubu enchaîné*, in 1900 (for details of the origin of this play and of *Ubu cocu* see *9*, chapter 5, and *1*, pp.466-84).

But publication was only half the battle. The play had also to be performed, on the live stage with professional actors and before a regular theatre-going public. From the beginning of 1896 onwards, Jarry waged an extraordinarily single-minded campaign for the staging of *Ubu Roi* which culminated in the riotous performance of 10 December 1896. Although the nominal director of the performance was the young Aurélien Lugné-Poe, who in 1893 had taken over the Symbolist Théâtre d'Art and renamed it the Théâtre de l'Œuvre which he had dedicated to the complete renewal of the existing theatre, it was in reality Jarry himself (who in the spring of 1896 had got himself appointed as the theatre's administrator and stage-manager and as Lugné-Poe's private secretary) who was not only the real moving force behind the production, but its virtual director. He it was who proposed and sought out potential actors for the parts; designed and ordered props; engaged the composer Claude Terrasse to compose and perform incidental music for the play; sounded out favourable critics and orchestrated a vast press-campaign generating advance publicity for the performance; and even on occasions, it would seem, conducted rehearsals in Lugné-Poe's absence. He also, in a stream of letters to the Œuvre's director, put forward a series of proposals for the production of the play which all modern directors would do well to meditate upon — the most important being contained in a letter of 8 January 1896 which it is worth quoting almost in full:

Il serait curieux, je crois, de pouvoir monter cette chose
(sans aucun frais du reste) dans le goût suivant:
1° Masque pour le personnage principal, Ubu, lequel
masque je pourrais vous procurer au besoin...
2° Une tête de cheval en carton qu'il se pendrait au cou,
comme dans l'ancien théâtre anglais, pour les deux seules
scènes équestres, tous détails qui étaient dans l'esprit de la
pièce, puisque j'ai voulu faire un "guignol".
3° Adoption d'un seul décor, ou mieux, d'un fond uni,
supprimant les levers et baissers de rideau pendant l'acte
unique. Un personnage correctement vêtu viendrait,
comme dans les guignols, accrocher une pancarte
signifiant le lieu de la scène. (Notez que je suis certain de la
supériorité "suggestive" de la pancarte écrite sur le décor.
Un décor, ni une figuration ne rendrait "l'armée polonaise
en marche dans l'Ukraine".)
4° Suppression des foules, lesquelles sont souvent
mauvaises à la scène et gênent l'intelligence. Ainsi, un seul
soldat dans la scène de la revue, un seul dans la bousculade
où Ubu dit: "Quel tas de gens, quelle fuite, etc."
5° Adoption d'un "accent" ou mieux d'une "voix"
spéciale pour le personnage principal.
6° Costumes aussi peu couleur locale ou chronologiques
que possible (ce qui rend mieux l'idée d'une chose
éternelle); modernes de préférence, puisque la satire est
moderne; et sordides, parce que le drame en paraît plus
misérable et horrifique. (pp.412-13)

I have attempted to provide a detailed reconstruction of the
performance of 10 December 1896 in chapter five. But a few
words must be said here about the play's reception and the
charges levelled against Jarry by spectators and critics. Both on
the evening of the performance and in the press during the days
and weeks that followed, three accusations in particular were
made. The first concerned the play's alleged vulgarity and
obscenity. Secondly, the play and its performance were con-
demned — perhaps inevitably, in view of the political climate of
the time — as a theatrical equivalent of the recent spate of

'anarchist' bomb attacks and as an act of anarchist-inspired political subversion. (Thus the figure of Ubu was seen by supporters and critics of the play alike as an embodiment of the 'bourgeoisie' and its alleged unscrupulous craving for and exercise of power.) The third accusation made against the play and its performance was that they in no way constituted a 'serious' piece of literature or of theatre, but simply a gigantic hoax.

Now, I think that there is an *element* — though in most cases only a tiny element — of truth in all of these charges. But most critics and spectators entirely missed the point of what Jarry was trying first and foremost to achieve. In fact, among both opponents and supporters of the performance there were few indeed who sought to judge it in purely artistic terms, as a piece of theatre. For Jarry himself, however, over and above the will to administer an enormous slap in the face to audiences of the day, the performance constituted both the projection onto the stage and the exposure to full public view of the haunting figure of Ubu himself, and an attempt to put into practice a new and quite revolutionary conception of the theatre. It is to an outline of that conception that we must now turn.

3. Jarry's Views on the Theatre

Jarry's writings on the theatre — though not in all cases easy to read since they are often written in the wilfully contorted, rather precious style popular among the Symbolists — are essential reading for anyone who wishes to understand fully his aims in the theatre. These writings are conveniently grouped together in the Folio edition of *Ubu* under the general heading of 'Textes autour d'*Ubu Roi*'. They comprise three published articles — 'De l'inutilité du théâtre au théâtre' and 'Les Paralipomènes d'Ubu', both of which appeared in the months preceding the performance of December 1896 and were intended as a preparation for that performance, and 'Questions de théâtre', which appeared in the *Revue Blanche* of 1 January 1897 and was intended by Jarry as a reply to his critics. To these must be added his unpublished article which appears in the above edition under the title of 'Réponses à un questionnaire sur l'art dramatique'; the text of his speech to the audience at the *première*; and the programme notes written by him which were published by the review *La Critique* and distributed to the audience on that occasion. Lastly, one must not overlook Jarry's letters to Lugné-Poe which contain his detailed proposals for a staging of *Ubu Roi*, published, with significant omissions which reveal even more clearly the full extent of Jarry's role in the production, in Lugné-Poe's memoirs (*20*) and in their entirety in *1*, pp.410-33.

The very title of Jarry's opening round in his attack on the existing theatre — 'De l'*inutilité* du théâtre au théâtre' — is a clear indication of the extent of his rejection of existing conceptions. A similar point is made in a passage from the Manifesto of the Théâtre de l'Œuvre for the opening of its fourth season in the autumn of 1896, almost certainly drafted jointly by Jarry and Lugné-Poe, which declared that 'si, dans le vocabulaire, un autre mot que le terme "théâtre" existait, nous l'aurions pris' (quoted by Lugné-Poe in *20*, p.170). What was this prevailing conception which had to be overthrown? To understand fully Jarry's intentions here, it is necessary to glance briefly at the state of the French theatre at the end of the nineteenth century.

The more superficial features of this theatre need not detain us here. Two essential characteristics however need to be stressed, the first of which concerns the status of the theatre in France during these years. It was essentially a Parisian phenomenon (there were more theatres in Paris alone than in the whole of the rest of France); it was almost exclusively a bourgeois institution; and it was essentially a theatre of entertainment, to which its bourgeois audiences went to be amused, delighted, rocked into gentle lethargy.[3] Though technically, in terms of the lavishness and splendour of its productions, at the most brilliant phase in its existence, in terms of its *artistic* value the French theatre had reached a nadir.[4]

Secondly, the French, and indeed European, theatre in this period was overwhelmingly a 'realist' theatre (one of which the 'naturalist' theatre of men such as Zola and Antoine can be seen, for our purposes, as simply an extreme development). The notion of realism is crucial to an understanding of the whole evolution of the novel, of the theatre, and even of painting, throughout most of the nineteenth century. It signified in general terms not only truth or accuracy of representation, but also the attempt to portray individuals as part of a concrete

[3] This at least was the predominant situation (if we except the efforts of Antoine at the Théâtre Libre between 1887 and 1894) at the time of the first production of *Ubu Roi*, though the situation was somewhat modified from the late 1890s onwards, particularly in the wake of the Dreyfus Affair, with the increasing vogue for socially critical dramas and 'problem plays'. See Wolfgang Asholt, *Gesellschaftskritisches Theater im Frankreich der Belle Epoque (1887-1914)*, Heidelberg: Carl Winter, 1984.

[4] Two details of this theatre (both of them the subject of reforms suggested by Jarry himself in his 'Réponses à un questionnaire sur l'art dramatique', p.319) will serve to underline the extent to which it had become a place of entertainment rather than a serious art form. It was still customary in most theatres at the end of the nineteenth century to keep the house lights on during performances, thus enabling members of the audience to look at each other as well as at the stage; and the doors of the auditorium remained open during the performance, thus allowing those same members of the audience to arrive (and to leave) as and when they wished!

social and historical situation, with great attention paid to the
authenticating details of the milieu in which they lived. In the
theatre, specifically, it involved the portrayal of psychologically
plausible characters whose behaviour and motivation could be
analysed and explained in terms of normal 'rational' criteria; a
coherent set of actions constituting the plot of the play which
resembled as closely as possible an episode from 'real life'; and
the creation of sets which endeavoured to recreate as con-
vincingly as possible the illusion of the world outside the theatre
— that of, for example, a real drawing room, or street scene, or
(in the case of one notorious production by Antoine) a butcher's
shop, the stage actually being bedecked with real sides of beef.
Implicit in the concept of realism, therefore, is the notion of an
essentially psychological and narrative theatre allied to a
particular mode of representation which seeks to create an
illusion of 'reality' in the material details of the stage itself. This
is a conception of the theatre which, among less artistically
aware audiences at least, is far from dead even today; but it is a
conception also which has been repeatedly called into question
by almost every serious theatrical reformer of the present
century.[5]

It is against the background of both these features of the
theatre of the nineteenth century that Jarry's own views and
activity must be seen. It is time to put to rest once and for all the
notion of Jarry as the *enfant terrible* of *fin-de-siècle* literature,
fiendishly setting out to *épater le bourgeois* and to engineer the
greatest theatrical hoax of all time. One has only to read his
writings on the theatre to be convinced of the seriousness of his
artistic aims and of his reforming zeal. Indeed, the article
'Questions de théâtre', written as a reply to the critics of the per-

---

[5] A discussion of the philosophical basis of this concept of realism, whose roots
are to be found in large measure in the nineteenth-century view of 'Science', and
of Jarry's no less philosophical reasons for rejecting both views, lies outside the
scope of the present study. It is worth pointing out however that his rejection of
the principles of realism in literature and painting goes hand in hand with a
detailed critique of the nature and pretensions of contemporary science,
expressed — albeit in deliberately paradoxical fashion — in his own 'science' of
pataphysics. In both of these fields Jarry was in the vanguard of a movement
which has led to a major critical and philosophical reappraisal in our own time.
For further details see *9*, chapter 7.

formance of *Ubu Roi*, is particularly revealing in this regard, through its tone of indignation and bitter resentment on the part of a much-misunderstood author. Alongside an admittedly real, but not exclusive, desire to shock and to outrage, Jarry shared with his Symbolist colleagues an almost religious reverence for 'Art' and wished fervently to restore to the theatre its one-time status as a serious art form. Indeed, he was closely involved in the early part of his literary career with Symbolism; and although he quickly outgrew the movement, spoofing some of its more extravagant manifestations in such works as *Les Minutes de sable mémorial* (1894) and *César-Antechrist* (1895), he continued to share such features of the Symbolist outlook as its aristocratic élitism, its deliberate anti-historical bias and its hostility to all forms of realism.

Of these shared views, none is more important in the present context than Jarry's and the Symbolists' resolute hostility to the artistic doctrines of realism and naturalism. He attacks in 'De l'inutilité du théâtre au théâtre' the banality of naturalistic themes and dramatic situations — 'des sujets et péripéties *naturelles* [*sic*], c'est-à-dire quotidiennement coutumières aux hommes ordinaires' (p.308, Jarry's italics) — and the hybrid and self-contradictory nature of supposedly realistic sets which are in reality 'ni naturel ni artificiel' (p.308). And in a curious passage in the programme notes distributed to the audience at the première of *Ubu Roi*, 'nature' and 'art' are explicitly declared to be opposites: the two terms form part of a series of antitheses which include respectively 'le moins de compréhension' (that is, the level of understanding of the ignorant and uncultured 'mob') and '[le] plus de cérébralité' (the intellectual state of the artist), 'la réalité du consentement universel' (that is, the 'common-sensical' view of the world held by 'the mob' based on the principle of induction which is the cornerstone of science) and 'l'hallucination de l'intelligent', 'les honneurs' (that is, recognition in the eyes of society) and 'la satisfaction de soi pour soi seul' (p.338).

What, then, is Jarry's alternative to the realist and naturalist theatre? He goes beyond the woolly-minded demands of a majority of the Symbolists for a 'poetic' theatre of mystery and

vague suggestiveness (which led even Lugné-Poe to perform the
naturalist dramas of Ibsen in a curiously unnaturalistic manner,
with actors moving about a dimly lit stage in a deliberately
stylized, 'mysterious' fashion) to formulate a number of more
precise demands. Three main aims can in fact be distinguished in
his writings on the theatre, and can be seen to be exemplified in
his detailed suggestions for the staging of *Ubu Roi*: the desire for
a theatre based on the principles of extreme simplification, and
even of 'abstraction'; the need for the theatre to concern itself
not with merely contemporary (and therefore ephemeral) but
with eternal and universal themes and preoccupations; and the
need for an overwhelmingly visual, as opposed to narrative and
psychological, theatre.

   The first of these aims can be seen most clearly in the article
'De l'inutilité du théâtre au théâtre' and in his 'Réponses à un
questionnaire sur l'art dramatique'. It is this desire for a
deliberately simplified, purely schematic representation which
lies behind and which explains his rejection of those elements in
a production which he regards as being too specific, which he
scathingly refers to as 'quelques objets notoirement horribles et
incompréhensibles ... qui encombrent la scène sans utilité', and
in the forefront of which he places 'le *décor* et les *acteurs*'
(p.308, Jarry's italics). The first of these two terms may not
cause us any surprise, since the use of purely schematic or symbolic props and sets has become a part of accepted theatrical
practice in the twentieth century. In the place of 'realistic' sets,
he argues in favour of a purely schematic or stylized backcloth
which will depict merely the 'substance' of a scene, or even
better a plain backcloth with the use of written placards to
indicate scene-changes. Any props that are needed, he maintains, can be brought on to the stage, in full view of the audience
(shattering in the process, of course, any illusion of reality) as
and when required — windows which need to be opened and
doors which are to be broken down just as readily as tables or
candlesticks (p.310).

   Jarry's relegation of the actor, however, to the status of a
mere 'object which uselessly encumbers the stage' may well take
us somewhat aback. Behind this attack lies in part simply a

reaction against the exaggeratedly elevated prestige of leading actors in the French theatre towards the end of the nineteenth century — lionized by fashionable society, having parts specially written for them, and dominating productions to the extent even, quite frequently, of choosing their own costumes. It arises in part also, however, from a widespread and deep resentment on the part of the creative writer of the freedom of interpretation (and therefore perhaps of distortion) which any actor enjoys — in part inevitably, since no actor can totally efface his own personality or physical appearance. Thus, Jarry argues, if human actors are to be used, then the actor should attempt to hide his individuality and human personality by wearing a *mask*, which will constitute 'l'effigie du PERSONNAGE' (p.310, Jarry's capitals) — different emotions or expressions being suggested by the play of light and shade upon the mask. In this way, the actor will become 'impersonal' — a point which Jarry stresses both in his speech to the audience at the première and in his programme-notes: 'Il a plu à quelques acteurs de se faire pour deux soirées impersonnels et de jouer enfermés dans un masque' (p.341), and the actors 'ont eu assez de talent pour s'oser vouloir impersonnels' (pp.338-39). Not only, moreover, should the individual physiognomy of the actor be suppressed, but his individual voice also — 'il va sans dire qu'il faut que l'acteur ait une *voix* spéciale, qui est la voix du rôle' (p.313) —, and his delivery must be deliberately monotonous, in the literal sense of the word. By these means the actor is to become merely a living puppet, 'un fantoche', or, as he explained it to the audience, 'l'âme des grandes marionnettes que vous allez voir' (p.341).

Certain of these ideas were undoubtedly specifically formulated, as Jarry himself admitted in a letter to Lugné-Poe of August 1896 (p.420), with a view to the staging of *Ubu Roi*. But they have for Jarry a more general import also. Such a conception of the theatre as that just outlined would result ultimately, he believes, in what he calls an abstract theatre — 'un théâtre ABSTRAIT' (p.316, Jarry's capitals) — something of which he believes he can see the beginnings in the work of a number of playwrights associated with the Symbolist movement,

such as Maeterlinck. The use of a purely schematic set, or even
more appropriately of a plain backcloth with settings and scene
changes being indicated by written placards, realizes in large
measure such an aim of abstraction, the written placard serving
to trigger off the imagination of the spectator who then 'sees'
the setting which seems to him most appropriate. Not only
deliberate simplification, moreover, but *naïve* simplicity — such
as that found in the paintings of his friend the 'douanier'
Rousseau, or in the actual set of *Ubu Roi* in 1896 — constitutes a
step on the path to abstraction: 'Le décor par celui qui ne sait
pas peindre [that is, according to the rules of academic painting]
approche plus du décor abstrait, n'en donnant que la substance'
(p.309).

This idea of abstraction has to be seen in the light of another
concept dear to Jarry, namely that of 'creation' in which the
audience itself will participate, and in the context, more
generally, of the Symbolists' insistence upon the primacy of
imagination. Instead of the playwright or the director
'imposing' a particular interpretation upon the mind of the
spectator through a too-explicit or too-specific representation,
the imagination of the spectator must be free to project its own
'meaning' or interpretation into the abstract or semi-abstract
framework provided. Thus, Jarry told the audience at the first
night of *Ubu Roi*, 'vous serez libres de voir en M. Ubu les
multiples allusions que vous voudrez' (p.341). In this way, the
élite of spectators to whom he addresses himself will be enabled
to participate *actively* in the process of creation, enjoying the
'plaisir actif de créer aussi un peu' (p.308). Indeed, it would be
dangerous for the 'poet' to impose upon 'un public d'artistes...
le décor tel qu'il le peindrait lui-même... Et il est juste que
chaque spectateur voie la scène dans le décor qui convient à *sa*
vision de la scène' (p.309). The audience's experience of the
theatre thus becomes not mere passive registering, but a form of
'action': the theatre itself is 'ni fête pour son public, ni leçon,
ni délassement, mais action' (p.317). Obscure though the
expression of such ideas in Jarry's writings may at times be, their
importance must not be underestimated: he is enunciating here
for the first time a concept of literature and of the theatre in

which the reader or spectator, instead of being a merely passive 'consumer', becomes in effect a 'co-creator' alongside the writer and/or director.

Two important sources of inspiration lie behind many of these ideas, sources which are to be found in the puppet theatre, and in contemporary developments in painting. Not surprisingly, Jarry found a model for the kind of theatre he wished to see created in the puppet theatre of his childhood. It was quite deliberately — if not wholly accurately — that in the original edition of *Ubu Roi* the title was followed by the words 'Drame en cinq Actes en prose. Restitué en son intégrité tel qu'il a été représenté par les marionnettes du Théâtre des Phynances en 1888'. And in his letter to Lugné-Poe of January 1896, he had pointed out that such proposals for the staging of *Ubu Roi* as the use of masks and of special 'voices' for the characters, as well as the schematic representation of crowds by a single actor, were in keeping with the *guignol*-like character of the play. Indeed, he was not alone among contemporary writers in seeing puppets as superior to the live actor, in their 'rudimentary', and therefore totally faithful, translation of the ideas of their creator, as he put it in a lecture on the puppet theatre given in Brussels in 1902 (*O.C.*, I, pp.420-23). But it is quite possible also that he was influenced by contemporary developments in the field of painting, in which he had a keen interest and a number of close friends — in particular amongst the 'Nabis', several of whom worked together on the set for *Ubu Roi*. By no stretch of the imagination can the work of the Nabis (or of any other painters of the period) be described as wholly abstract; but all practised a deliberately simplified and schematic style, which imparted to their work an air of deliberate unsophistication, or even of apparent crudeness or 'naïvety' — reminiscent, in a different medium, of the characteristics in the literary field of *Ubu Roi*. And it was moreover their chief spokesman, Maurice Denis, who in 1890 gave one of the classic definitions of the principles of non-representational art, to which ultimately such developments would lead: 'Se rappeler qu'un tableau — avant d'être un cheval de bataille, une femme nue ou une quelconque anecdote — est essentiellement une surface plane recouverte de couleurs en un certain ordre assemblées' (article in *Art et Critique*, 23 and 30 August 1890, cited in *8*, p.87).

The second of Jarry's demands, in his aim to transform radically the theatre of his time, was for a theatre which would concern itself with universal and eternal themes and pre-occupations — and thus also, by extension, with the creation of eternal archetypes and of 'myth'. Here too a parallel can be seen with the ideas of the Symbolists, and with those in particular of Mallarmé, a writer with whom Jarry has a number of close affinities. Both men see creation in the theatre not in terms of the invention of a plot or dramatic situation, but first and foremost in the conception of a character who will constitute a new *type*: for Jarry, to create means to 'faire naître un être nouveau' (p.319). And both men see an example of such an 'être nouveau' in Shakespeare's Hamlet: for Mallarmé, Hamlet is an embodiment of man's eternal adolescence, 'juvénile ombre de tous, ainsi tenant du mythe';[6] and Jarry, who sees in him a synthesis of various human characteristics, goes so far as to describe him as 'une abstraction qui marche' (pp.318-19).

Where Mallarmé was essentially a dreamer, however, at least in regard to the theatre, Jarry set about attempting to put such ideas into practice. Thus it is that Ubu himself constitutes his vision of Everyman. And the 'Nowhere' of the setting of *Ubu Roi* becomes, in conformity with the same principle, a universal Everywhere: 'Nulle Part est partout, et le pays où l'on se trouve, d'abord' (p.337). In practice, this universality is to be achieved in two ways. Firstly, the idea of simplicity itself is equated with universality: speaking of the facial expressions seemingly produced on the actor's mask by the play of the spotlights, Jarry maintains that 'comme ce sont des expressions simples, elles sont universelles' (p.312). Secondly, and perhaps more significantly, according to a theory dear to Jarry, facts which are mutually contradictory and deliberate incongruities cancel each other out, to produce a kind of universal and eternal void. Thus the costumes for *Ubu Roi* are to be deliberately incongruous and incoherent to stress the universality of the play's setting (pp.451-

---

[6] *Crayonné au théâtre*, in *Œuvres complètes*, Paris: Gallimard (Bibliothèque de la Pléiade), 1965, p.300.

53). The diction of the actors is to be similarly incongruous: according to the programme notes, Ubu speaks French, Bordure speaks English (that is, with an exaggeratedly English accent), Queen Rosemonde speaks in garbled Auvergnat dialect, and so on (p.337). And most strikingly of all, geographical and physical contradictions, together with historical or chronological contradictions (such as a pistol being fired in the year 1000 A.D.), cancel each other out to produce an abstract 'Nowhere/ Everywhere' and 'Eternity' respectively, as Jarry explained in an enigmatic passage of his speech to the audience describing the set for the original performance:

> Nous aurons d'ailleurs un décor parfaitement exact, car de même qu'il est un procédé facile pour situer une pièce dans l'Eternité, à savoir de faire par exemple tirer en l'an mille et tant des coups de revolver, vous verrez des portes s'ouvrir sur des plaines de neige sous un ciel bleu, des cheminées garnies de pendules se fendre afin de servir de portes, et des palmiers verdir au pied des lits, pour que les broutent de petits éléphants perchés sur des étagères. (p.342)

The third of Jarry's overriding aims — though one less emphasized than the preceding two — was to restore to the theatre its visual impact, in opposition to the largely narrative and psychological content of the theatre of his time. The true business of the theatre, he argues, is not to 'tell a story' — 'Toute "histoire" est si ennuyeuse, c'est-à-dire inutile' (p.322) —, nor is it the analysis of character, both of which aims belong more properly to the novel. Rather, the theatre should concern itself with the projection and visual manifestation of 'archetypal' *images* which will strike the imagination of the spectator and imprint themselves firmly on his memory. The point is made emphatically in a crucial passage in 'Questions de théâtre', which incidentally suggests a vision of Ubu as a wild monster about to be released on the stage:

> Je pense qu'il n'y a aucune espèce de raison d'écrire une

œuvre sous forme dramatique, à moins que l'on ait eu la
vision d'un personnage qu'il soit plus commode de lâcher
sur une scène que d'analyser dans un livre. (p.343)

More generally, Jarry's writings on the theatre reveal a strong
sense of the visual possibilities of the stage — of movement,
gesture and lighting, including an awareness of the expressive
possibilities of the newly invented electric spotlighting.

Such then are the key ideas put forward by Jarry in his
attempt to revolutionize the ideas of his contemporaries and
expressed in his various 'theoretical' writings on the theatre. For
all their intrinsic importance, however, their actual impact at the
time was, it must be admitted, minimal. Partly because those
who had the opportunity to read and to ponder on such ideas
formed a tiny section of the reading public, partly because the
alleged moral and political scandal of *Ubu Roi* drew attention
away from the extent to which the performance embodied a
purely aesthetic or theatrical revolution, it was to be many years
before the full importance of Jarry's place in the evolution of
conceptions of the theatre would come to be fully realized by
other than a tiny minority. Today, however, the importance of
Jarry's place in that evolution can at last be recognized, and a
number of detailed parallels can be seen to exist between his
ideas and the work of a good many more recent French
playwrights, as I have tried to show in the final chapter of this
study. And today too, with the text of Jarry's writings on the
theatre and of his letters to Lugné-Poe, which together contain
his own detailed proposals for a staging of *Ubu Roi*, easily
available in both French and English (see item *25* of bibliography) there is no longer any excuse on the part of would-be
producers and directors for ignorance of those ideas.

4. 'Ubu Roi': The Text

The examination in the previous chapter of Jarry's writings on the theatre should have served to show the seriousness of his artistic purpose. Yet time and again *Ubu Roi* has been seen in essentially or even wholly negative terms — as *simply* an attack, or a spoof, upon the existing theatre. At times, indeed, the play and its first performance have even been seen as the total negation of *any* possible form of theatre. Such is the view expressed, for example, by Denis Bablet:

> Jarry refuse le théâtre... *Ubu-Roi* [*sic*] est un guignol, c'est aussi la parodie du théâtre et c'en est la négation... Jamais on n'est allé aussi loin dans la négation de la logique inhérente au spectacle traditionnel... La représentation d'*Ubu-Roi*... propose un théâtre fondé sur la désintégration du théâtre et le démontage de ses rouages.
>
> (*8*, pp.166-67)

Up to a point Bablet is right: *Ubu Roi* certainly does deride every conceivable convention of the *then* existing theatre. But the play, and its original performance, represented also an attempt to escape from what its author saw as the impasse of realism and naturalism through the creation of an entirely new, and much more vital, form of theatre — as Henri Ghéon, invited by Jacques Copeau to outline his views on the theatre at the Théâtre du Vieux-Colombier in 1923, clearly saw:

> Savez-vous quel est, à mon sens, le titre principal de l'Œuvre à la reconnaissance des amis de l'art dramatique? La représentation d'*Ubu Roi*, dans un concert de cris d'oiseaux, de sifflets, de protestations et de rires; car j'y étais présent. ... Qu'on lui attribue le sens qu'on voudra, *Ubu Roi* de Jarry, c'est du théâtre "cent pour cent",

comme nous dirions aujourd'hui, du théâtre pur, syn-
thétique, poussant jusqu'au scandale l'usage avoué de la
convention, créant, en marge du réel, une réalité avec des
signes. (*Dramaturgie d'hier et de demain*, Lyon: E. Vitte,
1963, quoted in *11*, p.74)

Of the various principles and sources of inspiration outlined
in the previous chapter which lay behind this attempt at renewal,
none was more important for Jarry than the *guignol* or puppet
theatre, the chief characteristics of which have been nicely sum-
marized by Jules Bedner (*10*). In the traditional *guignol*, plot is
often anecdotal, psychology is rudimentary in the extreme,
tending to stylization and to caricature, whilst the action is
unbounded by limitations of time, space and logic. In short, the
world of the *guignol* (carrying on to some extent the traditions
of the *commedia dell'arte* and akin, in our own age, to the world
of the animated drawing or cartoon film) is a stylized fantasy
world with only minimal pretensions to being a copy of the real
world.

Jarry's originality in this respect was totally unrecognized by
almost all of his contemporaries. Even those who were dimly
aware of the *guignol* elements in the play and its performance
failed to realize their full significance; indeed, a number of
reviewers, while mentioning the fact that *Ubu Roi* was originally
'une farce de guignol', still tried to judge it in terms of such conventional dramatic criteria as coherence of plot, psychological
motivation of characters, plausibility, and the like. (The same
reproach can unfortunately be made of a number of more recent
studies also.) Yet Jarry's speech to the audience which preceded
the performance of 1896 contains no fewer than five allusions to
the art of the *guignol*, and in three of these he explicitly presents
the characters of the play as puppets (*marionnettes*). To adapt
Bergson's celebrated definition of comedy as 'du mécanique
plaqué sur du vivant' (*12*, p.50), we can say that the special and
unique quality of *Ubu Roi* arises above all from a super-
imposition of the characteristics of the puppet theatre or *guignol*
upon a subject, themes and dramatic framework belonging to
the traditional live theatre in its most serious, and even most

'noble' and 'heroic', forms. Whether or not such a super-
imposition was fully conscious on the part of the play's original
schoolboy authors, the fact remains that it is this factor which is
chiefly responsible for making of *Ubu Roi* a great comic play,
through the creation of an overwhelming and almost systematic
incongruity which is present at every level of the play, both in
the text and, as conceived by Jarry, in its staging.[7] In any study
of *Ubu Roi*, therefore, these two facts of the play's *guignol*
inspiration, and the deliberately derisory and parodic intention
which the work contains, must never be lost sight of. Together,
these will constitute the twin threads running through the
analysis of the play which follows.

(a) *Structure and plot*

On the face of it, there would seem to be a contradiction
between Jarry's professed contempt, seen in the previous
chapter, for considerations of plot and story-telling — para-
mount in the theatre of his day — and the actual structure of
Ubu Roi. The play does 'tell a story', that of the assassination of
a king and the seizure of power by one of his ambitious and
power-hungry lieutenants, followed by the progressive undoing
and eventual defeat of the tyrant. Indeed, the basic plot is that
of many an historical tragedy, of which Shakespeare's *Macbeth*
is probably the best known example. The division of the play
into five acts of roughly equal length, moreover, imitates the
formal structure of French classical theatre. And both within
each act, and within the play as a whole, there is a strong degree
of unity and coherence in regard to the development of the plot.

Act I functions as the exposition, outlining the plot to kill the
king and introducing the chief plotters and their victim, and
ending dramatically with the swearing of an oath to carry out the
deed. Act II shows the assassination of the king and two of his
sons and the flight of the remaining members of his family,
ending with Ubu at the apogee of his power being acclaimed by

---

[7] There is an irony in this situation which is nicely underlined by Henri Béhar:
'Ce n'est pas le moindre paradoxe que la liberté de conception de dramaturges de
quinze ans — ou, mieux encore, leur absence de réflexion — ait amené une
véritable révolution scénique' (*11*, p.50).

an enthusiastic and grateful populace (whilst also hinting at his subsequent undoing, the seeds of which are already present in his greed: such popularity as he has achieved is only the result of a feigned generosity and beneficence, designed to ensure his subsequent further enrichment). Act III shows the ferocity of Ubu's exercise of power and the growing crisis of revolt born of his excessive demands and depredations, ending once again with an appropriately dramatic climax as Ubu, at the head of the Polish army, sets off for war. The last two acts are, it is true, slightly less unified than the preceding ones. Act IV contains two episodes unconnected with the main plot, namely Mère Ubu's attempts to steal the treasure hidden in the crypt of Warsaw cathedral (Scene 1), and the episode of the bear (Scene 6). The main action of Act IV deals however with Bougrelas's recapture of Warsaw, followed by the engagement of the Polish and Russian armies leading to the eventual defeat and flight of Ubu. Act IV ends therefore with Ubu's fortunes at a nadir. The final act begins, somewhat curiously perhaps, with a continuation of the last scene of the preceding act, rendering the division into acts at this point unjustified in terms of the action; the main function of Act V however is to show the reuniting of Père and Mère Ubu, and their final escape from the pursuit of Bougrelas and his men as they set off for France to begin their adventures anew.

On first appearance, then, the action of *Ubu Roi* would seem to display a remarkable degree of unity. Indeed the progress and inexorable unfolding of a single plot is one of the dramatic strengths of the play. But this unity and coherence exist *only* on the level of plot. When we come to look at the number of different settings for the action, and the number of scene changes required, that unity comes to appear totally spurious, even derisory, and the structure of the play can be seen to constitute in reality a parody of the classical theatre. There are nineteen different settings for the action, including various rooms in a royal palace, a parade ground, two caves, a military encampment, a battlefield, and the deck of a ship. And there are no fewer than twenty-two separate changes of scene. The greatest number of these is to be found in Act III, where we move from an unspecified room in the royal palace in Warsaw, to the great hall of the palace, to a peasants' house in the Polish countryside, to a blockhouse in the fortifications of Thorn, to the Tsar's palace in Moscow, to Ubu's council room, and finally to the Polish army camp outside Warsaw. In no way can this rapid sequence of scene-changes be portrayed within the conventions of realism, or even with any degree of plausibility. The only manner in which such scene changes can be indicated is either through the use of an announcer or through the deliberately non-realistic, purely schematic technique of the use of written placards, befitting a puppet theatre, as Jarry himself had recommended. (It is worth noting also that chance plays a crucial, and totally implausible, role in Act V of the play, being entirely responsible for the reuniting, in a distant cave in Lithuania, of Père and Mère Ubu, and thereby rendering the play's 'happy ending' totally contrived.)

The same element of derision can be found also in the 'historical' content of the play, to which Jarry alluded paradoxically in a contemptuous remark in his programme notes of 1896: 'Nous ne trouvons pas honorable de construire des pièces historiques' (p.337). As the play demonstrates, there are more ways to avoid writing an 'historical' play than simply by avoiding history altogether. Many of the names of Jarry's characters did actually belong originally to real historical figures, as the researches of the editors of the Folio edition have shown (pp.456-59): there were at various times in the past and in various countries of central and eastern Europe rulers named Wenceslas, Ladislaw, Boleslas, Alexis, Mikhail Fyodorovich and Stanislas Leczinski (the last being king of Poland in the eighteenth century, father-in-law of the French king Louis XV, who took refuge in France and was made Duke of Lorraine). But by distributing these names indiscriminately as he does among Poles and Russians, kings and peasants, Jarry effectively achieves the result of that mutual cancelling out of anachronistic and contradictory elements to which he referred in a passage of his speech to the audience quoted in chapter three above.

A similar derisoriness can be seen in the treatment of time in the play. The latter presents the appearance of chronological unity and coherence, but in reality time is artificially telescoped. Events rush forward at breakneck and quite implausible speed, and the rapidity of transition from one scene to another is nothing short of farcical. Two examples will serve to demonstrate this. In Act III, Scene 3 we learn that news of Ubu's new taxation laws has just reached a peasant household in the Polish countryside; in the following scene Ubu is at the door of the house demanding payment of those taxes. And the scene of Ubu's visit to the now imprisoned Bordure in the blockhouse at Thorn (III, 5), which ends with Ubu's confident assertion that Bordure will never escape from his wretched prison, is immediately followed by that of Bordure's arrival at the court of the Tsar (III, 6). The improbable rapidity of the portrayal of events totally destroys any illusion of causal logic or coherence and renders the action derisorily comic, typical of the puppet theatre once again in its lack of realism.

Derision of or parody upon conventional dramatic forms is present, therefore, at every level of the structure of *Ubu Roi*. But in addition, both the plot of the play, and almost every one of its scenes, contain elements of parody either of traditional heroic or noble actions, scenes or motifs, or of the work of individual playwrights. In general outline, the plot of the play parodies that of almost all historical, and particularly royal, tragedies. As for individual scenes and motifs, the *balai innommable* of Act I, Scene 3 constitutes a parody of the royal sceptre; Ubu's battle with the Tsar (IV, 4) parodies many a stage battle; in place of the traditional noble steed, Ubu's horse is a feeble and ill-fed old nag; the false pathos of the death scene of Rosemonde (II, 5) parodies the traditions of popular melodrama; the no less false lyricism of Ubu's reflexions upon the death of Nicolas Rensky in battle (IV, 5) offers a spoof upon many a soliloquy on the subject of death; and Mère Ubu's unnaturally long monologue in Act V, Scene 1 parodies the tradition of the theatrical monologue.

Even more numerous are the elements of spoofing or parody upon the works of individual playwrights, in the play's plot, in the actions and gestures of its characters, and even in individual lines of dialogue, giving to *Ubu Roi* a quality of consistent and

all-embracing derision. The title, of course, parodies
Sophocles's *Œdipus Rex* (in French, *Œdipe Roi*). The plot in
general outline parodies that of Shakespeare's *Macbeth*: a loyal
servant of the king is egged on by his ambitious and
unscrupulous wife to murder the king and seize his throne, and
is eventually defeated by the son of the slain monarch. (The
Shakespearean source is hinted at, of course, by the facetious,
mock-Rabelaisian epigraph, which actually suggests an identity
— Shakes-peare = Hoche-poire — between Père Ubu and the
immortal Bard!) The hatching of the plot to kill the king in Act I
contains elements of parody upon Shakespeare's *Julius Caesar*
and in particular Corneille's *Cinna* (scarcely has the plot been
hatched when a messenger arrives from the king ordering Ubu to
appear before him (I, 5), just as Cinna is ordered to appear
before Augustus (I, 4)) whilst at the same time inverting the
situation in a number of important respects (Brutus and his
companions in Shakespeare's play plan to confront Caesar
openly, while Ubu is all for murdering Wenceslas by base and
stealthy means, and Cinna goes to face Augustus with a 'mâle
assurance', whereas Ubu behaves as a lily-livered coward). The
banquet scene in *Ubu Roi* (I, 3) may contain an allusion (though
under very different circumstances) to the banquet scene of
Macbeth (III, 4). The prophetic dream of Queen Rosemonde (II,
1) and her vain attempts to warn her husband of impending
danger constitute an obvious echo of the actions of Calpurnia in
Julius Caesar (II, 2). The scene in which Bougrelas is confronted
by the ghosts of his ancestors who charge him with the task of
avenging the brutal murder of his father (II, 5) contains an
obvious reference to the ghost scene of *Hamlet* (I, 5) with
perhaps a passing allusion also to the royal spectres conjured up
by the witches which file past the hero of *Macbeth* (IV, 1).
Hamlet is further recalled in Act V, Scene 4 of *Ubu Roi* by two
references to the town and castle of Elsinore. And a source for
the scene of the bear (IV, 6) has been variously found in
Shakespeare's *The Winter's Tale* and Molière's *La Princesse
d'Elide*. As to parallels in individual lines of dialogue, these are
far too numerous to allow more than a couple of examples to be
given. It has been noted that Ubu's exclamation in Act IV, Scene

4: 'Ah! Oh! Je suis blessé, je suis troué, je suis perforé, je suis administré, je suis enterré', recalls a similar outburst on the part of Harpagon in Molière's *L'Avare*: 'je suis perdu, je suis assassiné..., je me meurs, je suis mort, je suis enterré' (IV, 7). And Mère Ubu's line in Act V, Scene 1, which consists of an alexandrine and a half — 'Grâce au ciel j'entrevoi / Monsieur le Père Ubu qui dort auprès de moi' —, parodies (and imitates even in its spelling) a line from Racine's *Andromaque* (V, 5). (Further examples of such parallels are given by Henri Béhar in *11*, pp.62-63, several of them taken from a dissertation presented by Paul Jacopin at the Institut d'Etudes Théâtrales in Paris.)

Two further points need to be made about the structure of *Ubu Roi* which are quite unconnected with questions of parody. One might well argue that, in terms of the inherent logic of the plot, the play should end with Act V, Scene 3, which shows the final flight of the Ubus, and that the final scene of the original version, showing the Ubus on a ship heading through the Baltic for France, is unjustifiably 'tacked on' at the end. On the other hand, Scene 3 is far too short and insubstantial to provide a dramatically satisfying ending; whilst Jarry's aim is not to show the ultimate defeat of the tyrant Ubu — quite the contrary —, but merely the defeat of one particular scheme, leaving the Ubus free to carry on and to wreak havoc anew elsewhere.

Even so, the fact remains that the conclusion of Act V, Scene 4 also is dramatically rather weak, ending as the scene does on a feeble joke made by Ubu himself. It may well have been for this reason that Jarry chose to end the marionette performances of the play given to resounding applause at the Théâtre des Pantins in January 1898 with the *Chanson du Décervelage*. This was subsequently included in the third and final edition of the play, published jointly with *Ubu enchaîné* by the Editions de la Revue Blanche in 1900, which is reproduced in the Folio edition. The consequences of this inclusion are however mixed. On the one hand the song, marvellously entertaining in itself, particularly if sung to the music composed by Claude Terrasse, does provide a resounding finale to a performance of the play (all the more so if the audience happens to know the song and, as in pantomime performances, joins in). On the other hand, the addition of the

Chanson du Décervelage (which belonged originally to the group of fragments, rather different in character and mood, from which *Ubu cocu* was eventually composed) radically alters the atmosphere of the play and its performance, rendering it much more jovial, and modifying the tone of derision and parody. It was presumably in recognition of this that, in one of the two (otherwise identical) printings of 1900, the titles of the two plays are followed by the word 'Comédie'. Was this an implicit admission by Jarry that, after the first performance of 1896, *Ubu Roi* had inevitably lost some of its power to shock and scandalize, and that it was necessary to accentuate its comic elements? Depending on the nature of audiences, modern directors may feel inclined to agree.

(b) *Characters and characterization*

The two strands of derision and of the inspiration of the puppet theatre are to be found every bit as much in the characters of *Ubu Roi* and in Jarry's techniques of characterization as in the play's plot and structure. It is utter foolishness to attempt to subject the play to the sort of psychological analysis which one might apply to more conventional plays and to seek for coherence and complexity of character and motivation. Time and again we find a disproportion or incongruity between action and motives, cause and effect, ends and means.

Jarry's characters are in fact Punch-and-Judy-type figures, and their psychology is as deliberately rudimentary as that of the puppet theatre; motivation is simplified in the extreme, and everywhere characterization takes the form of caricature, the taking of a limited number of character traits or physical features and exaggerating them to ludicrously improbable proportions. Thus, the Tsar is the embodiment of high-minded nobility and valour; Wencelas of generosity and gullibility; Bougrelas of filial piety and courage; Queen Rosemonde of noble virtue and lucidity. The very names of the *dramatis personae* embody these elements of caricature and parody. What could seem to the popular imagination a more fitting name for a caricatural king of Poland than Wenceslas? As for Wenceslas's

three sons, Ladislas, Boleslas and Bougrelas, the rhyming
ending of each name together with the obscene implications
contained in the last (which is of course a creation by Jarry himself) clearly point to their deliberately derisory nature. Bordure
inevitably calls to mind *ordure*, though it (together with the
names of the three *palotins*, Giron, Pile and Cotice) is in origin a
term from the language of heraldry.[8]

The name Ubu, on the other hand, is a case apart, suggesting
something at once comic and sinister. The repetition of the
vowel sound introduces a mildly comic resonance, as in all such
similarly fabricated names. But the word as a whole has the sug-
gestion of something primitive, monstrous and grotesque about
it which renders it unforgettable. The magnificent resonance of
the name, in fact, probably has a good deal to do with the fame
of Jarry's creation; for even many people who have never seen
or read the play and know next to nothing about it do know the
name Ubu.[9]

---

[8] All four heraldic terms admit of a 'sexual' interpretation with overtones of
pederasty, *bordure* (the border or surround of an escutcheon or heraldic shield)
and the other three terms (all representing pointed or elongated shapes) signi-
fying the sphincter and the male sexual organ respectively. These and many other
possible sexual significances which can be seen to derive from the intertextual
links which Jarry established *a posteriori*, implicitly or explicitly, between *Ubu
Roi* and a number of his other works are outlined in great detail by Michel Arrivé
in *6*. Whilst there is no denying the brilliance of Arrivé's analysis and the evident
polysemy of much of the vocabulary of *Ubu Roi* when considered in a wider
semiological context, it has to be emphasized that none of this has any bearing
upon a consideration of the play *as a play*. Although Charles Morin was over-
stating his case when he claimed that *Ubu Roi* was 'la pièce la plus chaste *in the
world*' (*sic*, quoted by Chassé, *13*, p.30), it is nonetheless true that sexual
allusions are minimal, and wholly derisory, in the play, and the relationship
between Père and Mère Ubu is in no way a sexual one. Ubu is emphatically *not*
an embodiment of lust, any more than are the other characters in the play, and
any attempt to introduce such considerations runs entirely counter to Jarry's
own intentions.

[9] Of the various explanations of the origin of the name, by far the most con-
vincing (notwithstanding Jarry's own rather spurious derivation from the Greek
ybex, 'vulture'), and from several points of view the most satisfying, is that put
forward by J.-H. Sainmont in *22*, p.61. In the original Lycée de Rennes version
of the *Chanson du Décervelage*, published by Chassé (*13*, pp.86-89) under the
title *Tudé*, there occurs the refrain:
>   Voyez, voyez la machine tourner,
>   Voyez, voyez la cervelle sauter,
>   Voyez, voyez les rentiers trembler,
>   Hurrah, cornez au cul, vive le P.E. [*var.*: le Père Ebé].

Ebé (or *le P.E.*) here formed a disappointingly weak rhyme with *trembler* until,
in Sainmont's hypothesis, Jarry hit upon the idea of making the name rhyme

The character who bears that name is, of course, the central and dominant figure in the play, around whom everything, in accordance with Jarry's theory of dramaturgy, revolves. Of the play's thirty-three scenes, Ubu is present on stage in all but seven. He is also the only character in the play, apart perhaps from Mère Ubu, who displays more than two or three basic character traits. (I do not propose to examine the character of Mère Ubu as such, since she appears merely as a lesser version of her hideous husband, and, after her initial role as temptress, makes no further contribution to the main plot of the play.) Ubu has so often been seen as the embodiment principally, or even solely, of greed, or lust for power, or tyranny, or even (heaven forbid!) lasciviousness, that it is necessary to examine the character as he appears *in the text* of the play in order to determine what precisely his chief characteristics are. It is impossible to put these in an exact order of importance, since a number are equally important or overlap. I shall however save for discussion last what seems to me to be Ubu's most dominant character trait.

The feature which strikes us first is Ubu's unashamed vulgarity, symbolized in the oath — 'merdre' — with which the play begins. This vulgarity is abundantly manifested in both word and deed — verbally, in the oft-repeated oaths with which the text is studded, in Ubu's assertion that he has 'un cul comme les autres', or in his crude statement that 'j'en fais dans ma culotte' (V, 2); and, through his actions, in his brandishing of the lavatory brush in Act I, Scene 3, or his inability to control his bowel movements both during the battle scene and in the final confrontation with Bougrelas. Though important, this vulgarity is by no means the dominant feature of the character, however, and productions of the play which unduly add to the vulgarity and would-be obscenity not only distort Jarry's intentions, but risk becoming tedious as well.

with *cul*, thus giving to this splendid classical alexandrine an internal rhyme between the two hemistichs. The explanation has the merit of stressing the link between Ubu and his *cul*, that is the furthest extension of his *gidouille* or belly which is his most salient characteristic — a point emphasized by Jarry in 'Les Paralipomènes d'Ubu' speaking of Plato's 'three souls': 'Des trois âmes que distingue Platon: de la tête, du cœur et de la gidouille, cette dernière seule, en lui, n'est pas embryonnaire' (p.323).

Also present from the beginning is the aggressiveness of the
character, which quickly takes the form of sadistic cruelty. Ubu
repeatedly proffers threats of violence, first and foremost
against his wife, and subsequently against all and sundry. He
delights in the spectacle of smashed skulls as his newly acquired
subjects fight each other for the gold which he throws them, and
gleefully runs through the list of the various tortures to which he
will subject his victims. This sadistic brutality reaches a peak in
the execution of the Nobles, Magistrates and Financiers in Act
III, Scene 2, where Ubu's ferocity appals even his hideous and
bloody spouse.

The converse of this aggressiveness and cruelty is Ubu's lily-
livered cowardice, which is closely allied to his fickleness and
treachery. He repeatedly expresses fears of being struck blows
('recevoir des coups') or of being kicked; whilst his behaviour
during the battle against the Russians, and later in the encounter
with the bear, is an example of ignoble cowardice in the extreme.
No less striking is his treachery: he twice threatens to denounce
his fellow plotters to the king when he believes their assassination plot has been uncovered, imprisons his former ally
Bordure once he no longer has need of him, and treacherously
flees the battle zone while the commander of his troops, General
Lascy, is not looking (IV, 4). Yet all of this is shown, once again,
in deliberately derisory terms; Ubu's reaction upon learning of
the planned invasions of his lands by Bordure and the Tsar is
typical:

> Ho! ho! J'ai peur! J'ai peur! Ha! je pense mourir. O
> pauvre homme que je suis. Que devenir, grand Dieu? Ce
> méchant homme va me tuer. Saint Antoine et tous les
> saints, protégez-moi, je vous donnerai de la phynance et je
> brûlerai des cierges pour vous. Seigneur, que devenir? (*Il
> pleure et sanglote.*) (III, 7)

Two further important characteristics are Ubu's gluttony and
his greed, or more exactly avarice. References to food abound —
indeed it is amongst other inducements the prospect of being
able to eat lots of *andouilles* (chitterlings) that persuades Ubu to

agree to the assassination plot; and, following his seizure of the throne, Act III begins characteristically with the words: 'De par ma chandelle verte, me voici roi dans ce pays. Je me suis déjà flanqué une indigestion'. We also witness his gluttony in the banquet scene of Act I, where he steals the food intended for his guests. (In this connection, the physical appearance of the character is important: he *must* be portrayed as enormously fat. And although it is not essential for Mère Ubu to be excessively thin, such a portrayal does provide an effective visual contrast.) Alongside this gluttony, the idea of self-enrichment is repeated numerous times throughout the play, expressed in such statements as 'je veux m'enrichir' (II, 6) and 'Eh! je m'enrichis' (III, 2), and provides one of the chief motivating forces behind Ubu's behaviour. Indeed, it is ultimately Ubu's avarice which proves to be the chief source of his undoing.

It is in this context that we need to see the portrait — and it is a caricatural one — which Jarry gives us of absolute tyranny in Act III, Scene 2. This is the central scene of *Ubu Roi* structurally, it is one of the longest, and it is also, to my mind, the most brilliantly effective scene of the play dramatically. Whereas up to this point Ubu has simply been king with unspecified powers, here we see him enjoying a situation of absolute power, as he takes over all property and titles following the execution of the Nobles, all legislative and judicial capacity following the execution of the Magistrates, and finally all financial power as a result of the execution of the Financiers. Small wonder that Ubu has often been seen as a Hitler- or Stalin-like figure (or has been compared also to such bloody petty tyrants as Idi Amin, or Papa Doc, or Bokassa), concentrating all power in his own hands, with appalling consequences. Indeed, he can be seen as embodying the terrifying absurdity of such a situation. There is a line spoken by him in Act III, Scene 4 which Jarry obviously considered to sum up so well the character and significance of Ubu that he used or quoted it, or a variation upon it, in two others of his early works, *Les Minutes de sable mémorial* and *César-Antechrist*: 'Avec ce système [i.e. of taxation] j'aurai vite fait fortune, alors je tuerai tout le monde et je m'en irai'.[10] Ubu's words sum up the ultimate absurdity of the exercise of truly absolute power: for when the tyrant has appropriated unto himself or otherwise destroyed everything, what else is there for him to do but... 'go away'?

To an extent, then, such an interpretation of Ubu as the embodiment of absolute power is justified. But two crucial facts have to be borne in mind, which modify this perspective. The first is the extremely caricatural, and utterly derisory, nature of this usurpation and exercise of power — as shown, for example, in the patent absurdity of the all-powerful tyrant having himself to go from village to village to collect taxes, or having personally to force couples to marry in order to collect the newly instituted marriage tax. The second is that this accumulation of titles and offices of which Ubu's power is constituted is not the fruit of a lust for power for its own sake, which is the mark of the true tyrant, but a means to an end, born of Ubu's basic greed and avarice, of his desire for self-enrichment.

There is one further and final trait of Ubu's character which also modifies the potential sinisterness of Jarry's portrait, and which is in fact his dominant characteristic — namely, his childish stupidity. This stupidity is manifest from the very outset of the play, in Ubu's failure to understand the drift of his wife's promptings (in fact, twice in the first dozen or so lines of the play he frankly admits to not understanding a thing). And not only do we continue to see evidence of his utter stupidity in Ubu's every word and action, but the other characters repeatedly comment upon that stupidity far more often than upon any other of his character traits. The dialogue is studded with such comments as 'Tu es si bête' (I, 1), 'il est imbécile' (I, 3), 'Quel sot homme' (III, 7), 'Il est vraiment imbécile' (III, 8), all uttered by Mère Ubu, and 'Est-il bête, ce Père Ubu' (I, 6) and 'Quel triste imbécile' (V, 4), spoken by Bougrelas and Pile respectively. As for Ubu's childish nature, time and time again we see evidence of this in the text. His dearest wishes are for

---

[10] In *Les Minutes de sable mémorial*, where the quotation stands alone preceded simply by the words, 'Ubu parle', this idea was formulated even more starkly: 'Quand j'aurai pris toute la Phynance, je tuerai tout le monde et je m'en irai' (*O.C.*, I, p.241).

simple things — to eat lots of *andouilles* and to have a big *capeline* (wide-brimmed hat) such as he used to have in Aragon, or an umbrella, or a *grand caban* (cloak). In gratitude for the title newly bestowed upon him by Wenceslas, he offers the king a *mirliton* (reed pipe or whistle). And when he thinks of denouncing his fellow conspirators, he believes that the king would in return give him some pocket-money ('de la monnaie'). Not only is Ubu's own psychology and behaviour throughout characterized by such childlike naïvety and childish stupidity, moreover, but the whole perspective in which the events of the play are presented to us is similarly one of childlike simplicity. Ubu embodies a kind of primeval innocence which is terrifying in its implications; but he is also — as the title 'Père' prefixed to the name Ubu suggests — first and foremost a comic character, laughable in his childishness and utter stupidity.[11] This childish stupidity underpins all of his other characteristics and renders Jarry's portrayal of his gluttony, his avarice, his cruelty and his tyranny an essentially comic, and derisory, one. It is difficult to hate that which makes us laugh; and evil rendered comic loses its ability to arouse indignation. This is a point which is all too often overlooked, but which ought never to be forgotten in any interpretation of the play.

(c) *Ubu, a satirical figure?*

The above discussion leads on directly to a question which has been the subject of much debate and misunderstanding — namely, is Jarry's intention in *Ubu Roi* primarily satirical, and if so what does the play satirize? Satire — different in this respect from mere spoofing or parody — is an essentially aggressive form of humour which, whilst attacking certain values or forms of behaviour, implicitly affirms their opposites. It also tends to have a *specific* social, or political, or moral goal, implying that an alternative to those values or attitudes is possible. Is this the case with *Ubu Roi*?

The play has certainly been seen many times over in terms of

[11] The title 'Père' prefaced to a name implies familiarity which may be tinged either with endearment or slight contempt. Judith Cooper is quite wrong however in asserting (*14*, p.77) that it 'heightens the impression of vulgarity'.

satire. A passage from a review of the original performance by
Catulle Mendès, quoted in part by Jarry himself in 'Questions de
théâtre' and quoted many times over since, is a typical case in
point. Mendès sees the figure of Ubu as being made up 'de
Mayeux et de M. Joseph Prud'homme, de Robert Macaire et de
M. Thiers' — all embodiments of the archetypal bourgeois,
swindler or scheming politician — and sees the play as a whole as
an attack upon 'les pudeurs, les vertus, les patriotismes et l'idéal
des personnes qui ont bien dîné' (p.430). A similar view was
shared by almost all of Jarry's contemporaries, who insisted
upon seeing the play in terms of political and social satire, as an
attack upon the legendary 'bourgeois'. And it has been per-
petuated right down to the present day, faithfully echoed for
many years by the popular *Petit Larousse illustré* on which many
generations of Frenchmen have been brought up and which,
right up until its 1985 edition, continued to define *Ubu Roi* as a
'comédie caricaturale, satire énorme de la bourgeoisie' and to
define the character of Ubu *simply* as a 'caricature bouffonne de
la stupidité bourgeoise'.

Is this really, however, what emerges from the text itself? It is
perhaps just possible, by a stretch of the imagination, to see
elements of satire in a number of scenes of the play, for example
upon the greedy, grasping 'bourgeois' of popular legend in a
statement such as Ubu's 'Eh! je m'enrichis. Je vais faire lire MA
liste de MES biens. Greffier, lisez MA liste de MES biens' (III, 2),
or upon the hypocrisy of certain self-interested practitioners of
virtue in Ubu's words 'Je suis tout disposé à devenir un saint
homme, je veux être évêque et voir mon nom sur le calendrier'
(V, 1). But if such barbs are directed against the supposed
'bourgeois', the lower orders are treated with no more respect,
being shown as ignorant, greedy, brutal and fickle. The point is
nicely made in a comment by Luc Decaunes which takes a side-
swipe at the capacity for self-deception of generations of French
intellectuals:

Faire d'*Ubu roi* une dénonciation féroce de la bourgeoisie
serait une illusion auto-suggestive, car le peuple n'y est pas
ménagé davantage. Ni psychologique, ni politique, ni

sociale, à cent lieues de la comédie de mœurs comme de la
satire de tel ou tel régime, la farce... pose en fait la
négation de toutes les "échelles de valeur".[12]

In fact, in all these examples the caricature is so gross as to rob
them of any value as effective satire, rendering such allusions
totally derisory.

What of Jarry's views expressed in his various articles and
other writings? It is true that once or twice he allowed himself to
be carried along by the enthusiasm of Ubu's supporters in the
direction of a socio-political interpretation, and equally true that
he intended the audience to see in the monstrous figure of Ubu a
reflection, or the 'double', of itself:

> J'ai voulu que, le rideau levé, la scène fût devant le public
> comme ce miroir des contes de Mme Leprince de
> Beaumont, où le vicieux se voit avec des cornes de taureau
> et un corps de dragon, selon l'exagération de ses vices; et il
> n'est pas étonnant que le public ait été stupéfait à la vue de
> son double ignoble... (p.344)

But the very terms of this analogy make it clear that he conceived of the character of Ubu in moral rather than socio-
political terms, and elsewhere he protested vigorously against all
such interpretations in terms of social and political satire. In
'Les Paralipomènes d'Ubu', he warned in advance against any
over-simplistic anti-'bourgeois' interpretation, and pointed
clearly to a conception of Ubu in universal and moral terms:

> Ce n'est pas exactement Monsieur Thiers, ni le bourgeois,
> ni le mufle: ce serait plutôt l'anarchiste parfait, avec ceci
> qui empêche que nous devenions jamais l'anarchiste
> parfait, que c'est un homme, d'où couardise, saleté,
> laideur, etc. (p.323, Jarry's italics)

At the performance itself, in his speech to the audience, whilst

[12] 'Jarry tel quel', in TEP [= Théâtre de l'Est Parisien] Actualités, October
1974.

thanking those critics who had written favourable previews of
Ubu Roi, he was moved to protest that 'leur bienveillance a vu le
ventre d'Ubu gros de plus de satiriques symboles qu'on ne l'en a
pu gonfler pour ce soir' (p.340); indeed, he gave as his justification for making this speech the very need to make such a
protestation. And although, somewhat ambivalently, in this
same speech he did allow the audience the right to interpret the
play as it wished — 'vous serez libres de voir en M. Ubu les
multiples allusions que vous voudrez' (p.341) —, in his programme notes distributed to the audience on the same occasion
he denied all responsibility on his own part or on that of the
actors for all such views, implying that the universal and eternal
setting of the play — its mythical Nowhere/Everywhere —
rendered invalid all interpretations in terms of a specific
country, or historical period, or social class: 'Si diverses satires
se laissent voir, le lieu de la scène en fait les interprètes
irresponsables' (p.337).

In reality then, as the setting for the action suggests, Ubu
represents quite simply Jarry's version of Everyman — vulgar,
cruel, cowardly, gluttonous, avaricious, and above all stupid.
That Jarry's vision is a particularly grim and pessimistic one —
embodied in a figure whose prototype already represented for
him, at the age of fifteen, 'tout le grotesque qui fût au monde'
(p.341) — is undeniable. But equally undeniable is the
imaginative power of that vision (and, it must be stressed, of
that *comic* vision) of human baseness. Here, at least, we must
agree with Mendès when he wrote:

> Le Père Ubu existe... Vous ne vous débarrasserez pas de
> lui; il vous hantera, vous obligera sans trêve à vous
> souvenir qu'il fut, qu'il est; il deviendra une légende
> populaire des instincts vils, affamés et immondes. (p.430)

(d) *Language and verbal humour*

The language of *Ubu Roi* is striking both for its colour, its
vigour and its inventiveness, on the one hand, and for its
deliberate incongruities on the other. Both sets of features are

among the chief sources of humour in the play. It was a total
failure to appreciate the true nature of the play's humour which
accounts in part for the audience's reaction in 1896, and which
led to accusations of hoaxing on Jarry's part. Most members of
the audience had gone to the theatre in the expectation of being
treated to a display of jokes and witty remarks, particularly in
the form of sexual innuendoes; and they came away feeling frustrated. Yet, as Jarry himself made clear in 'Questions de
théâtre', there was absolutely no reason to expect a character as
patently stupid as Ubu to come out with successful jokes and
witticisms ('des mots d'esprit') (p.345). On the contrary, almost
all the jokes (with perhaps one exception) which Ubu tries to
make are stupid and pathetically feeble, as the other characters
do not hesitate to tell him — that is they are, like so many other
features of the play, deliberately derisory. And any attempt to
produce *Ubu Roi* along the lines of a verbally witty play
complete with music-hall-type jokes and snide remarks constitutes a total travesty of Jarry's intention and of the spirit of the
text.

Nothing exemplifies more vividly, and more fully, the
characteristic features of the language of *Ubu Roi* than the
play's opening word, *merdre*. It embodies at one and the same
time the vulgarity and obscenity of much of the play's language;
its violence and aggressiveness; the element of linguistic
deformation and invention; and the numerous elements of
mystification which the text contains. Let us look at each of
these features of the language of *Ubu Roi* in turn.

The opening *merdre* typifies and sums up the verbal obscenity
and vulgarity contained in the play. Not only was its use in *Ubu
Roi* in 1896 the first time the word had ever been used on the
modern French stage, but its position and the force of its
delivery gave it the maximum possible prominence in the performance, vastly intensifying its impact. The word occurs a total
of thirty-three times in the course of the play, including twenty-
one times as an oath or exclamation, either alone or in combination with other terms. It also occurs with considerable force in
the multiple oath 'bougre de merdre, merdre de bougre', where
the word *bougre* — in certain contexts harmless enough (*un bon*

bougre, for example, means simply 'a good fellow') — takes on a highly obscene and vulgar significance. And it is used with considerable effect also in the terms of address 'madame de ma merdre', directed to Mère Ubu (III, 7), and 'garçon de ma merdre', directed to the messenger Nicolas Rensky (IV, 3). Expressions such as 'cul' (I, 1), 'foutre le camp' (I, 6), 'je vais sûrement crever' (I, 6), and the delightful 'je me suis ... crevé la bouzine' (I, 6) where the element of word-creation (*bouzine* = 'dung-bag') adds to the comic effect, all reinforce the vulgarity or obscenity of the play's language. Yet the very exaggeration of the use or repetition of such terms causes this element of obscenity and vulgarity to go deliberately 'over the top', revealing Jarry's intention once again to be one of derision rather than a serious aim to shock.

The same applies to the violence and aggressiveness inherent in the opening 'merdre' (which was followed in the text of the original edition by an exclamation mark), and in the play's language generally. The curtain rises in Act I, Scene 1 of the play on a heated exchange between the two main protagonists, and logically the word must be addressed to Mère Ubu; but by its position and force, the audience is made to feel that the word may be directed at it as well or instead. The word 'merdre' is Ubu's automatic response to any situation in which his will is frustrated or thwarted, and the expression of his desire simply to smash down any obstacles in his way. That same aggressiveness is expressed also in a string of terms used both by Ubu himself and by others — *sagouin*, *bourrique*, *charogne*, *chipie* — and in a series of colourful threats of violence. Mère Ubu is threatened with beating (I, 1), having her eyes torn out (I, 2) and Ubu's teeth sunk into her calves (I, 3), and being torn to pieces (III, 1). Others are threatened with being killed or with unspeakable tortures, the longest and most detailed list of which is promised to Mère Ubu in Act V, Scene 1:

> torsion du nez, arrachement des cheveux, pénétration du petit bout de bois dans les oneilles, extraction de la cervelle par les talons, lacération du postérieur, suppression partielle ou même totale de la moelle épinière..., sans

oublier l'ouverture de la vessie natatoire et finalement la
grande décollation renouvelée de saint Jean-Baptiste...

A number of these threats of violence are of an amusingly
culinary nature, adding to the colour and inventiveness: 'vous
allez passer... par la casserole' (I, 1), 'En compote les
Moscovites!' (IV, 4), 'Je vais te faire cuire à petit feu' (IV, 4);
and, typically, Ubu assaults Bordure's henchmen in the banquet
scene with 'côtes de rastron' (I, 3). The violence and aggressiveness of the characters expresses itself also in several long lists of
insults, characteristic of the play's verbal exuberance generally.
These reach a climax in the final confrontation between
Bougrelas and the Ubus in Act V, Scene 2:

> BOUGRELAS, *le frappant*: Tiens, lâche, gueux, sacripant,
> mécréant, musulman!

> PÈRE UBU, *ripostant*: Tiens! Polognard, soûlard, bâtard,
> hussard, tartare, calard, cafard, mouchard, savoyard,
> communard!

> MÈRE UBU, *le battant aussi*: Tiens, capon, cochon, félon,
> histrion, fripon, souillon, polochon!

The verbal fantasy displayed here in these long lists of rhyming
insults is typical of the play as a whole, in which a tendency
exists for language to become self-generating and to lose all
touch with any recognizable reality. In the example quoted,
although it is possible to see tenuous associations at a couple of
points (the juxtaposition of *Polognard* and *soûlard* recalls the
expression 'soûl comme un Polonais', whilst *mécréant*, taken in
the sense of a non-believer in Christianity, might just possibly
suggest *musulman*), on the whole the words become simply
autonomous blocks of sound which are metaphorically hurled at
the adversary, the rhyme reinforcing this quality and simultaneously pointing to the derisory nature of the supposed
insults.

The third element inherent in the word 'merdre' is that of
linguistic deformation and invention. The addition by Jarry (or

by the pupils of the Lycée de Rennes, since it is certain that the
word goes back to the play's schoolboy origins) of an extra *r* to
the celebrated *mot de Cambronne* gives it a magnificent
resonance far beyond that of its original form (*merde*), which it
is, alas, impossible to recapture in English. Far from
euphemizing the word however (as the somewhat prissy substitution of *mince* for *merde* in French, or *sugar* for *shit* by some
English-speakers, seeks to do), the purely derisory nature of
Jarry's apparent camouflage gives to the word instead a parodic
value, caricaturing a popular form of linguistic deformation and
substitution. This linguistic deformation and inventiveness,
moreover, is an important factor in enlivening the play's string
of oaths and obscenities; for vulgarity and obscenity quickly
become tedious unless constantly renewed by imagination and
invention.

The process of linguistic invention can be seen at work also in
a whole series of composite oaths or other terms. A number of
these — the terms *machine à décerveler*, *Pince-Porc*, *Chambre-
à-Sous* — were discussed in chapter two. Then there are the
appendages of the Nobles referred to in Act III, Scene 2: the
caisse à Nobles, *crochet à Nobles*, *couteau à Nobles* and
bouquin à Nobles. Most such linguistic creations are however
associated with Ubu himself, their number increasing markedly
in the scenes in which he is king, doubtless as a result of the need
to list his regal attributes and appendages. These tend to fall into
three groups. The first is that associated with his role as 'Maître
des Finances' (or 'Phynances') and involve his quest for *finance*
or *phynance* (Jarry uses both spellings indiscriminately) — the
sabre à finances (III, 1, III, 3, III, 7), *salopins de finance* (III, 4,
a survival from Charles Morin's original version of the play,
Jarry elsewhere changing *salopin* to *palotin*), *voiturin à
phynances* (III, 4), *croc à finances* (or *phynances*) (III, 8, IV, 1,
IV, 4), *cheval à phynances* (III, 8), *casque à finances* (IV, 3),
pistolet à phynances (IV, 3), and the *Chanson à Finances* (IV, 3)
sung by his loyal followers. The second group, mostly referring
to Ubu's instruments of aggression, comprises those composites
with the word *merdre* — the *sabre à merdre* (III, 8, IV, 4), *croc à
merdre* (III, 8, IV, 3), *ciseau à merdre* (IV, 3) and *sac à merdre*

(V, 1). The last is constituted by those oaths or exclamations incorporating the word *corne*, in which it is possible to see (through association with the horns supposedly worn by a cuckold) an attenuated sexual implication — *cornegidouille* (by far the most frequent form, which Jarry defines in his pro-gramme notes of 1896 as meaning 'par la puissance des appétits inférieurs' (p.338)), *cornefinance* (III, 5), *corne de ma gidouille* (III, 7), *corne d'Ubu* (III, 7, III, 8), *corne physique* (III, 8) and *cornebleu* (IV, 2, IV, 3, no doubt by analogy with *ventrebleu*, etymologically *ventre de Dieu*). It is interesting to note that the frequency of the exclamations 'merdre' (which occurs fourteen times in Act I and seven times in the first scene alone) and 'de par ma chandelle verte' decreases markedly in the later part of the play, and particularly in those scenes where Ubu rules as king, being to a considerable extent replaced from Act III, Scene 3 onwards by 'cornegidouille' and its variants. Other instances of verbal inventiveness are the *ciseau à oneilles* and *couteau à figure* (both in III, 8) which, together with the *petit bout de bois*, are among Ubu's panoply of torture instruments, the potentially obscene *jambedieu* (IV, 3, IV, 4, V, 1) borrowed from Rabelais, the *bâton à physique* (IV, 3) which plays an important role both in the sexual symbolism of Jarry's *César-Antechrist* and in his demonstration of the 'identity of opposites' (a central concept of his 'science of pataphysics'), the various terms used to designate Ubu's belly or gut — *gidouille, giborgne, bouzine, boudouille* —, the verb *pocher* derived from Ubu's *poche* or *pôche*, and the use of such pseudo-baby-language forms as *oneilles*.

The fourth and final feature of the language of the play embodied in its opening 'merdre' is the element of mystification, or hoaxing, which it contains. At the original performance of *Ubu Roi* in 1896, according to the novelist Rachilde, Jarry's deformation of the word provoked the audience to even greater heights of fury than would have otherwise been the case since, failing to understand either the reason for or the significance of that deformation, it felt that on top of an apparent insult it was being hoaxed into the bargain! The same element of hoaxing can be seen in Jarry's retention in the text of a number of terms or allusions which derive from the original schoolboy folklore of

Rennes and which are quite incomprehensible to all but its
initiates — among them the recurrent exclamation 'de par ma
chandelle verte', which occurs twelve times in the play, the
play's allusions to Aragon and to the Spanish, the 'côtes de
rastron' of the banquet scene (I, 3), Ubu's threat to the others
that they will 'visiter [ses] poches' (I, 7), the mysteriously
exploding *palotin* of Act II, Scene 2, and the 'chiens à bas de
laine' referred to in Act III, Scene 7. Despite what has been said
previously about the fundamental seriousness of Jarry's artistic
purpose, there is evidence here of an undoubted will to mystify
his audience. But times and attitudes have changed, and where
the spectators of 1896 reacted with fury born of frustration, a
modern audience is more than likely simply to laugh at such
incomprehensible allusions. Our age has learned to live with,
and even to find a source of enjoyment in, the absurd.

Apart from the features of the play's language outlined
above, there are also a number of forms of linguistic incongruity
which are a source of humour. The first of these is the juxtaposition of different registers within the dialogue, and even
within individual lines of dialogue. Three typical examples can
be found in the opening lines of the play. The first occurs in the
first line spoken by Mère Ubu: 'Oh! voilà du joli, Père Ubu,
vous estes un fort grand voyou', where there is an incongruity
between the colloquialism 'voilà du joli' and the falsely archaic,
pseudo-Rabelaisian 'vous estes'. The second is to be found in
Père Ubu's retort: 'Que ne vous assom'je, Mère Ubu!', where
the very formal inversion introduced by *que* contrasts strangely
with the violence of the verb *assommer*. And a third occurs in
the assurance by Mère Ubu to her husband: 'vous pourriez faire
succéder sur votre fiole la couronne de Pologne à celle
d'Aragon', where the formal construction *faire succéder* is used
alongside the slang term *fiole* (noddle). There is also Ubu's
curious habit of lapsing on occasions into apparent baby-
language: 'ji vous mets dans ma poche' (III, 4), 'Ji tou tue' (III,
8), 'Ji lon mets dans ma poche' (III, 8) and 'ji lon fous à la
poche' (IV, 5). Equally incongruous, and so also, it would seem,
equally arbitrary, is the frequent alternation of the two terms of
address *tu* and *vous* in the dialogue both between Ubu and his

wife and in the lines spoken by Wenceslas (I, 6) and the Tsar
(III, 6) — the inconsistency of usage, incidentally, creating a
deliberate inconsistency of character also.

The greatest incongruity of all, however, is that between
language and context or situation. It goes without saying that no
king, however much of a coarse tyrant, ever spoke as does Ubu.
Whilst the language and style of the Tsar, Wenceslas and the
latter's family make a *pretence* of being appropriately elevated
and noble, the discordance could not be greater between the
language of the Ubus and the situation to which they aspire and
which they usurp. Examples of this abound in the text and help
to give it much of its comic resonance. One is that already
quoted in which Mère Ubu eggs her husband on with the words
'vous pourriez faire succéder sur votre fiole la couronne de
Pologne à celle d'Aragon', which is followed a few lines later by
the statement: 'A ta place, ce cul, je voudrais l'installer sur un
trône'. As examples of the advantages he would enjoy as king,
she tells Ubu: 'Tu pourrais augmenter indéfiniment tes richesses,
manger fort souvent de l'andouille et rouler carrosse par les
rues', and a few lines later: 'Tu pourrais aussi te procurer un
parapluie et un grand caban qui te tomberait sur les talons' (I,
1). At the beginning of Act III, there is an exchange between the
Ubus typical in its ludicrous over-simplification of the situation:

PÈRE UBU: De par ma chandelle verte, me voici roi dans ce
pays. Je me suis déjà flanqué une indigestion et on va
m'apporter ma grande capeline.

MÈRE UBU: En quoi est-elle, Père Ubu? car nous avons
beau être rois, il faut être économes. (III, 1)

And after despatching all the Nobles, Ubu characteristically
announces: 'je veux faire des lois maintenant' (III, 2). Examples
of other instances of incongruity between language and situation
also abound. Ubu's assertion in Act I, Scene 1 that he has 'un
cul comme les autres' is in blatant defiance of the visible truth.
Ubu addresses the king simply as 'monsieur Venceslas' (I, 6),
and replies to the latter's formal invitation: 'Noble Père Ubu,

venez près de moi avec votre suite pour inspecter les troupes', with the colloquial 'On y va, monsieur, on y va' (II, 2). And what could be more incongruous than Ubu's celebrated remark to his wife at the beginning of the banquet scene: 'Mère Ubu, tu es bien laide aujourd'hui. Est-ce parce que nous avons du monde?' (I, 2)? Finally, there is the sheer illogicality of Ubu's remark in Act IV, Scene 6, as he is seeking for means of cooking the bear: 'Je vais allumer du feu en attendant qu'il apporte du bois'.

(e) *Action and gestural humour*

Alongside the verbal humour in the play, much of the comedy derives also from the purely schematic or truncated nature of events and the improbable rapidity with which those events unfold. Both these features are characteristics of the puppet theatre, and it is in respect of the action and use of gesture in the play, rather more than of the language, that *Ubu Roi* remains closest to its puppet origins. The truncated and improbably rapid unfolding of events is so obvious as barely to need demonstrating (although it is perhaps more easily realized in watching a performance than in reading the play). Within a matter of minutes the seeds of the assassination plot are sown, the plot is hatched, and the king is murdered. No sooner has Ubu seized the throne than he sets about at breakneck speed massacring the Nobles, Magistrates and Financiers. And no sooner has he announced his new taxes than he is seen busy collecting them and wreaking havoc and destruction as he goes. And so the action rushes on. The momentum is on the whole unrelenting (although it is true that the action slows down somewhat in parts of Act IV and at the beginning of Act V, making of these the least entertaining moments of the play), and performances of the play must maintain this momentum if its full comic potential is to be realized.

There are plenty of examples to be found also of a use of action and gesture which in some respects may seem more appropriate to the puppet theatre than to the live stage, and which add enormously to the liveliness and enjoyment of the play in performance. A number of events partake of the slap-stick and knockabout comedy of traditional farce — for example, the action of Ubu in almost smashing in his chair with his enormous bulk (I, 3, implied by the line: 'Ouf, un peu plus, j'enfonçais ma chaise'), Ubu flinging himself upon Bordure in order to embrace him (I, 4), Ubu falling helpless on the ground as he goes to take leave of the king (I, 6), Ubu falling off his horse as he sets off for battle (III, 8), and, just possibly, the scene of the killing of Wenceslas (II, 2), as Ubu stamps on the king's foot and the others hurl themselves upon him, then set off in pursuit of his sons. But certain other elements of the action and gestural language of the play cry out to be performed in an extremely stylized or purely schematic fashion, typical above all of the puppet theatre. Examples of this are the exploding *palotin* of Act II, Scene 2, Bougrelas splitting the skull of a soldier and 'massacring' a crowd of others as he whirls around with his sword like a windmill followed by his 'unstitching' of Ubu (II, 4), the appearance of the ghosts of Bougrelas's ancestors in the mountain cave, the 'carnage épouvantable' effected by the *palotin* Giron amongst Bougrelas's supporters (IV, 2), Ubu 'tearing apart' his enemies in battle (the stage directions several, times read 'Il le déchire'), the scenes with the bear (IV, 6 and V, 1), and finally the scene on the ship crossing the Baltic (V, 4). There are also the various crowd scenes, in particular the race in Act II, Scene 7, and the battle scenes in Act IV, for the second of which Jarry suggested the deliberately incongruous use of a *single* soldier. Above all else, the scene in which Ubu's adversaries are consigned to his *trappe* (III, 2) is an example of a brilliantly comic scene which can most effectively be portrayed in an extremely brusque, mechanical, puppet-like manner. A final puppet-like element is provided by having a number of lines spoken simultaneously and in chorus by two or more of the characters. Thus Bordure's henchmen exclaim in unison such lines as 'Vive la Mère Ubu', 'Eh! nous n'avons pas dîné' and 'je suis mort!' (all in I, 3), 'Fi, le sagouin!', 'Oui! voilà qui est noble et vaillant' and 'Conspuez le Père Ubu!' (I, 7). The Queen and Bougrelas simultaneously cry out 'Quelle erreur' (II, 1) and later fall on their knees and exclaim together 'Mon Dieu, défendeznous' (II, 3). Other examples are provided by the choruses of Magistrates and Financiers in Act III, Scene 2, and by Mère Ubu and Pile exclaiming in unison in the final scene 'Délicieuse chose que la navigation'. In all these instances the deliberately unnatural unison creates a mechanical effect which accentuates the puppet-like character of the dialogue and action and provides a source of a great deal of humour.

Systematic exploitation of incongruity in both language and gesture, therefore, is a major source of comedy in *Ubu Roi* — the chief source, in fact, exceeding in importance even the elements of parody and spoofing, and the technique of exaggeration to ludicrously improbable proportions typical of traditional farce. But the greatest incongruity of all, of course, lies in the fact of human actors performing roles originally conceived for marionettes. The inhuman, mechanical nature of actions, gesture and diction which this transposition imposes (or should impose) upon the performance is an unending source of comedy — a procedure nicely summed up by Jarry's one-time philosophy teacher, Henri Bergson: 'Les attitudes, gestes et mouvements du corps humain sont risibles dans l'exacte mesure où ce corps nous fait penser à une simple mécanique', in which 'on nous fait voir dans l'homme un pantin articulé' (*12*, pp.30-31). However successful a performance of *Ubu Roi* may be as a puppet play, paradoxically its success when performed by human actors on the stage of the live theatre is even greater — *provided* that it is performed in as mechanical and puppet-like a manner as possible.

Two final points need to be made concerning this aspect of the play's comedy. The first is that Jarry, going beyond the traditional techniques of farce and word-play to a systematic exploitation of incongruity and the creation of what we might call a form of 'absurd' humour, far outreached the expectations of his contemporaries, to become a trail-blazer and a prophet of our own age. (Precisely *why* we should laugh at such forms of humour, where the audience of 1896 responded with baffled incomprehension and outrage, is of course another question.) The second point concerns the ultimate aim of the comedy of *Ubu Roi*. In contrast to the analysis of Bergson, who saw humour as having essentially a socially and morally corrective function, stigmatizing departures from an accepted 'norm' of behaviour, the humour of *Ubu Roi* is 'metaphysical' rather than moral in intent (and in this respect also constitutes a portent of our own age). Far from having any morally corrective intention, Jarry, in his comic portrayal of the grotesqueness and stupidity of his monstrous creation, Ubu, is quite simply inviting us to laugh — and to laugh heartily — at ourselves and the grotesque monstrosity of our own lives.

(f) *Myth and childhood vision*

In his various writings on the theatre, Jarry had called for the creation of a theatre dealing not with purely contemporary, and therefore ephemeral, issues, but with eternal and 'archetypal' themes and situations. He argued also for a theatre which, rather than 'telling a story', would concern itself with the projection of imaginatively powerful and compelling images. *Ubu Roi* realizes both these aims perfectly. In it, Jarry has presented us with his own *image* of Everyman, and has attempted to create a powerful and eternally valid 'myth'. Such an image — seeming to present mankind as a whole as crass, vulgar, treacherous, cruel, brutal and stupid — reveals of course a particularly bleak and pessimistic view of the world, one which implicitly subverts all humanistic belief in the inherent goodness and rationality of man. Here is no doubt a further reason for the violent reaction of Jarry's contemporaries to the play, in which — in Jarry's view — they saw, but refused to acknowledge, the portrayal of their 'ignoble double'. For the play seemed to attack both their most cherished artistic conventions and their moral image of themselves. Today, in our post-Freudian age, more fully aware of the darker side of the human psyche and convinced by the devastating experience of two World Wars and their associated horrors of the forces of latent aggression buried within the human subconscious, we are perhaps more willing to accept the image which Jarry offers us of ourselves in the figure of Ubu — and to rise above it by laughing at it, and at ourselves. Ubu constitutes an appropriate and compelling 'myth' for our own times.

But whilst offering us a powerful image and 'myth' of
Mankind itself, Jarry's play expresses a vision of another kind
also. There is an indisputable logic of a sort in Mère Ubu's argu-
ment that 'si tu ne fais pas de distributions, le peuple ne voudra
pas payer les impôts' (II, 6), or in Ubu's reassurance following
the execution of the Financiers: 'Ne crains rien, ma douce
enfant, j'irai moi-même de village en village recueillir les impôts'
(III, 2), or in the latter's assertion in the final scene of the play
that 'S'il n'y avait pas de Pologne il n'y aurait pas de Polonais'.
And nothing could be more incontrovertible than the terrifying
logic of his statement: 'Avec ce système j'aurai vite fait fortune,
alors je tuerai tout le monde et je m'en irai' (III, 4). But this
'logic' reveals a childlike simplicity of perspective which
characterizes not only such statements as these, but indeed the
whole play. The logic of events is that of the grossly over-
simplified and simplistic view of the world of the child, and Ubu
himself has all the characteristics of an overgrown child. At the
same time, the element of verbal fantasy, the enjoyment of
playing with the sound and the shape of words, is a characteristic of childhood also. Even without a knowledge of the play's
origins, it is impossible to imagine *Ubu Roi* as anything other
than a product of childhood, a creation of an exuberant, unruly
and disrespectful schoolboy imagination. This is an aspect of the
work which the audience of 1896 almost totally failed to
appreciate, products as its members were of an age of High
Seriousness, in which the adult world felt itself obliged to hold in
contempt the productions of childhood. (Indeed, Jarry shrewdly
observed in *Ubu enchaîné* that 'ce qui fait rire les petits enfants
risque de faire peur aux grandes personnes'.) The reaction of
modern audiences, however, is likely to be quite different. For
today, ninety years on, we are much more willing to recognize
the value of that feeling of delight in the nonsensical and the
absurd out of which the play was born. It is perhaps the greatest
of all Jarry's claims to fame that he alone, amongst his school
fellows and contemporaries, saw the value of this naïve,
grotesque yet fascinating and delightful work of childhood,
perceiving in it qualities commensurate with the highest art.

5. Performances

More than most plays, *Ubu Roi* is a work which cries out to be seen and heard on the stage if its full potential is to be realized — which perhaps explains the disappointment felt by some readers when confronted simply with the text. The purpose of this chapter is therefore to give a brief account of a number of noteworthy past performances of the play. The list of performances discussed in no way pretends to be complete: I have concentrated for the most part, of necessity, on performances given in France and Britain; and my aim throughout has been not so much historical as designed to show the differences of approach to the play displayed by different producers and directors. I have also attempted to offer some assessment of the relative merits of each, basing myself on the two criteria of theatrical effectiveness and of authenticity, that is conformity to the spirit of the text and to Jarry's own basic intentions (some may argue that this is not a criterion that matters, though I happen to believe that it is). Where possible, the descriptions and assessments are based on my own experiences and recollections, but I have supplemented these where appropriate by information from contemporary critical accounts, newspaper reviews, and interviews with or writings by the directors concerned. A selection of photographs of performances can be found in *9* and *11*.

The first, and most notorious, of all the performances of *Ubu Roi* was of course that given at the Nouveau Théâtre by Lugné-Poe's Théâtre de l'Œuvre in December 1896, which was the occasion for one of the greatest uproars which the French theatre has ever seen. Two performances of the play were actually given if we include, in addition to the riotous première of 10 December, the dress rehearsal the previous evening which was attended largely by an audience of fellow writers and artists on the whole sympathetic to the play. The two are frequently confused in the minds of writers of memoirs and occasional reminiscences; it seems to have been the second of the two which created the greater scandal, though in other respects the following comments apply to both performances.[13]

The set was the work of a team of artists, regular collaborators of the Théâtre de l'Œuvre and present or future friends of the playwright himself — Sérusier, Bonnard, Vuillard, Toulouse-Lautrec and Ranson. In place of the 'plain' backdrop originally proposed by Jarry to Lugné-Poe, they had actually produced a painted backdrop which combined extreme simplification and stylization with the juxtaposition of the most heterogeneous and contradictory elements, a work in which contemporaries saw the ultimate expression of the then fashionable artistic doctrine of 'syntheticism' but which constituted also a deliberate *reductio ad absurdum* of all forms of realism. The single most detailed description has been left by a visiting British critic, Arthur Symons:

> the scenery was painted to represent, by a child's conventions, indoors and out of doors, and even the torrid, temperate and arctic zones at once. Opposite to you, at the back of the stage, you saw apple-trees in bloom, under a blue sky, and against the sky a small closed window and a fireplace... On the left was painted a bed, and at the foot of the bed a bare tree, and snow falling. On the right were palm-trees, about one of which coiled a boa-constrictor; a door opened against the sky, and beside the door a skeleton dangled from a gallows. (*27*, p.373)

On the window, which surrounded a few gently undulating hills,

---

[13] A great deal of confusion prevails concerning the reception of the play at each of these two performances. Claude Schumacher (*24*) asserts categorically that it was the performance at the *répétition générale* on 9 December which gave rise to the greater disturbance, basing himself, seemingly, on the accounts of Jarry's biographer Noël Arnaud (*Alfred Jarry d'Ubu Roi au Docteur Faustroll*, Paris: La Table Ronde, 1974) and of the actor playing Ubu, Firmin Gémier (interview in *Excelsior*, 4 November 1921). But Arnaud's account is carefully ambiguous in regard to this question, whilst Gémier's reminiscences twenty-five years later are contradicted by other eye-witnesses. The truth *seems* to be that the play was generally well received at the dress rehearsal until towards the end of Act III, when the situation suddenly degenerated and chaos ensued, whereas at the première audience hostility was manifested and interruptions occurred right from the very beginning of the performance.

perched a number of owls; to one side an elephant sat astride a huge red disc representing the sun; a chamber-pot was clearly visible beneath a yellow-curtained bed; and the black marble fireplace in which a fire burned opened down the middle to allow the actors to enter and to leave the stage. The whole of the action took place against this single unchanging backdrop, scene changes being indicated by placards which were brought on to the stage and suspended from a nail by a tall black-suited individual with long white hair and beard. The props were hardly less schematic: a bale of straw on the floor of the stage signified a prison cell; to represent the Nobles, Financiers and Magistrates consigned to Ubu's *trappe* in Act III, life-sized wickerwork *mannequins*, appropriately costumed, were used, forty of which Jarry had ordered and had delivered to the theatre, together with a life-sized pantomime-style *cheval à phynance* for the equestrian scenes. As for the costumes, which he had suggested to Lugné-Poe should be as lacking in 'local colour' as possible in order to suggest more accurately the idea of something 'eternal', these appear to have combined, according to observers,[14] everyday banality with elements of deliberate incongruity (such as trousers rolled up to the thighs) which were no doubt intended to produce the same mutual cancelling-out effect to which Jarry had referred in his speech to the audience when describing the set. Jarry also had made a huge cardboard and wicker belly, which was worn by Gémier, the actor playing Ubu.

More significantly, the actors themselves, or at least those playing the leading parts, were masked, Gémier wearing, somewhat reluctantly, the heavy pear-shaped or triangular mask designed by Jarry which the latter had forced upon him — a

[14] The chief source of information here is Victor Mandelstamm, quoted in *Cahiers du Collège de 'Pataphysique*, 20 (1954), p.52, and by François Caradec in *L'Etoile-Absinthe*, 7-8 (December 1980), pp.66-69. There survives also a list of detailed instructions concerning costumes written in Jarry's own hand which point in the same direction (though there is no way of knowing the precise extent to which these instructions were carried out): Ubu is to wear a steel-grey suit, with a walking stick in his right-hand pocket and a bowler hat on his head which is topped by a crown when he becomes king, Mère Ubu is to be dressed as a concierge cum wardrobe dealer, Bordure is to be dressed as a Hungarian gipsy musician, Bougrelas is to wear a baby's dress and bonnet, and so on. The full text can be found in *1*, pp.451-53.

means of hiding the individual personalities or features of the actors which aroused indignation in many critics in an age in which the actor reigned supreme. Each adopted a distinctive 'voice' or accent, as suggested by Jarry: Gémier imitated the brusque, staccato diction learned from Jarry himself which embodied, according to Lugné-Poe, a conception of Ubu as a 'machine à broyer les humanités' (*20*, p.176) very different from the Ubu-clown of a number of subsequent performances; whilst Louise France as Mère Ubu spoke in a form of *patois* (dialect), the actor playing Bordure spoke with an English accent, the Tsar with an exaggeratedly Russian accent, Queen Rosemonde with an Auvergnat accent, and others, according to critics, with Belgian or Alsatian accents. And the actors were also made to attempt, as far as was possible, to imitate in their bearing and movements the stiff and jerky actions of marionettes, much to the disgust and bewilderment, once again, of many critics. Incidental music for the performance — described by Symons as fairground music befitting a puppet play (*27*, p.372) — was provided by the composer Claude Terrasse. Most interesting of all was the use of a deliberately stylized and schematic mode of representation on the part of the actors themselves, which included even a use of actors to replace props. A single actor was used to 'represent' the Polish army in Act IV and in other scenes involving crowds, including the military review of Act II, the race of the final scene of the same act and the battles of Act IV, as Jarry had advocated. The *palotins*' descent of a hill was suggested by their moving across the stage behind a screen which hid the lower half of their bodies, progressively bending their knees until their heads disappeared behind the screen, their ascent being suggested by the same movements in reverse order. And in the scene in which Ubu pays a visit to the imprisoned Bordure (III, 5), an actor with arm outstretched was used to represent the door of the prison cell, Gémier pretending to insert a key into his hand, making a clicking noise, and swinging the arm as if opening a door (an action which, curiously, provoked a tumult of protest which continued to the end among the audience at the dress rehearsal, so utterly wedded were Jarry's contemporaries to 'realistic' modes of representation). In such 'signes susceptibles de suggérer ce qu'on ne pouvait montrer' and 'actions en raccourci et très expressément synthétiques', the critic Romain Coolus, almost alone, in an article in the *Revue Blanche* of 1 January 1897, saw 'une sorte de langage théâtral nouveau'.

The above description applies, at least, to those features of the performance which corresponded more or less to Jarry's own intentions. But in a number of significant respects the performance escaped his control. Inadequate rehearsals had forced a number of cuts to be made, mainly, it seems, in Act IV, in those scenes involving the bear, to the resentment of Jarry himself to judge by his bitterly ironical comments in his speech to the audience. Above all, the actors, whose role should have been reduced to that of mere automata performing their marionette-like gestures at the command of an invisible puppet master, assumed a quite unforeseen and independent role as a result of the uproar created by the performance: in order to quieten the audience and to transform protest into laughter, Gémier and Louise France resorted to dancing jigs or improvising pantomime-like scenes on the stage, and Gémier blew into a horn similar to that used by omnibus or tram drivers, diversions which on the whole succeeded in subduing the public for a time. Indeed, Lugné-Poe in his memoirs presents the performance at the first night as a uniquely spontaneous event made up of the conjunction of the scandalized reactions of the audience, the impromptu 'inventions' of the actors and the *ad hoc* musical accompaniment of Terrasse, which by its very nature could not be repeated (*20*, p.178), something akin to the impromptu 'happenings' of Dada.

Such accidents apart, however, the fact remains that in three essential respects the performance was in accordance with the intentions of the author and unofficial director — namely, in its stress upon the play's violence and verbal truculence; in its systematic exploitation of incongruity for comic effect in set, costumes, acting and diction; and in its adoption of schematic or merely 'symbolic' modes of representation, deriving in part from the art of the mime and the puppet theatre, which were diametrically opposed to those of the realist and naturalist theatre but which constituted, in Henri Ghéon's words, an outstanding example of 'pure' theatre. It was, alas, to be many years more before the same qualities were to be fully realized in a performance again.

A revival of the play at the Théâtre Antoine in March 1908, four months after Jarry's death, was the first in a long line of productions which in one or more crucial respects betrayed the intentions of the playwright himself. Gémier once again played the lead role, but was now also in charge of the production and able to fashion it to his own ends. The set comprised a backdrop painted according to a child's conventions, with doll's house, geometrically regular lawns and neatly conical trees, and a vaguely Slavonic palace in the background, described by one critic as being 'd'une naïveté voulue', but lacking the flagrant incoherence and incongruity of the original set of 1896. Scene changes were once again indicated by the use of placards which reproduced Jarry's own stage directions — 'Palais du roy', 'Une table splendide est dressée', and the like. Props were relatively simple and few, and included a pantomime-like horse with two men inside it. Surviving photographs show the Tsar as a muzhik-like figure, with peasant's tunic and cap and bushy black beard, emerging like a jack-in-the-box from a large wooden crate marked 'LE CZAR — Fragile'; Bordure with cotton-wool hair and goatee beard, and with tassels attached to his joints as a marionette would have; and Wenceslas with a placard suspended from a chain around his neck bearing the word 'ROY'. Mère Ubu however — played, interestingly, for the first time by a man, Bougrelas being in turn played by a woman — was all frills and flounces and made up rather like a circus clown; whilst Gémier's large pot-belly, frock-coat, flabby false cheeks and conical bald skull, reminiscent of the pear-shaped head of popular caricatures of King Louis-Philippe (he refused this time to wear the heavy mask which Jarry had formerly imposed upon him), gave him a vaguely avuncular air, on which was superimposed a satirical note by his wearing of a modern cavalry uniform in the battle scenes. To Jarry's text and conception of the play, a good many jokes and gags had been added, including a strange introductory scene and an even stranger ending: at the

start of the performance Père and Mère Ubu arrived from oppo-
site sides and trotted towards the centre of the stage where they
collided violently with each other, fell down dazed, then
returned in the direction whence each had come to the
accompaniment of childish mutterings and wild gestures; and at
the end all the characters, both living and dead, stood together
in a line on stage and fell asleep, snoring! Although in some
respects the performance appears rightly to have stressed the
naïve and childlike elements in the play's conception, on the
whole the impression is one of knockabout fun and jokiness in
place of the violence and studied incoherence of 1896.

No further revivals occurred in Paris until 1922 when Lugné-
Poe, having finally reconciled himself to the play and profiting
from the renewal of interest provoked by Chassé's revelations
the previous year, once again staged it at the Théâtre de
l'Œuvre. Here too, however, reactions to the performance were
muted, to say the least, though its failings were not wholly
attributable to Lugné-Poe himself who was absent from Paris
during preparations, leaving rehearsals to the direction of René
Fauchois, the actor playing Ubu, in whose hands, as Lugné-Poe
later admitted, 'la pièce glissa ... vers la farce d'atelier. La satire
ne porta pas; la vigueur cruelle, féroce, échappa au public'.[15] A
number of important changes were made to Jarry's text:
extensive cuts were made, mainly in Acts IV and V; and,
curiously, each of the five acts was given a title, some of these at
least being inspired by recent or contemporary events and
alluding to elements of the set or briefly mimed scenes which
occurred alongside and parallel to the main action of the play.
Placards were once again used to indicate scene changes, aug-
mented on occasions by cardboard or wooden cut-outs of
buildings etc., placed on stage to the accompaniment of brief
musical interludes or blackouts. Other props too were brought
on stage or removed during the musical interludes, in view of the
audience. The 'eccentricities' of the production were on the
whole appreciated by critics, who found them agreeably

[15] *La Parade*, III: *Dernière pirouette*, Paris: Le Sagittaire, 1946, p.143, quoted
by Ruth B. York, '"Ubu" revisited: the *reprise* of 1922', in *French Review*, 25
(February 1962), p.409.

amusing, together with the music of Terrasse which was once again used; but the rest of the performance was greeted with indifference on the part of critics and audiences alike, and did little if anything to enhance the reputation of Jarry or the standing accorded to the play.

Indeed, the performance may have actually done harm, for it was another twenty-three years before *Ubu Roi* was again performed in Paris, in the wake of the ending of the Second World War, first by the young Compagnie Guy Renaud under the direction of Archibald Penmach in April 1945 and then at the Théâtre du Vieux-Colombier in November 1946. Once again the reception of critics and public was cool. The reasons for this would seem to lie both in a lack of forcefulness in the two performances, and in the nature of the historical context. Robert Kemp in *Le Monde* (8/9 April 1945), reviewing the first performance, maintained that the reason for its lack of impact lay in the nature of recent political reality which far surpassed in horror anything that Jarry had imagined, a view with which a number of other critics appeared to agree. Others felt that, despite the use in both productions of a suitably stylized or schematic set (together with, in the first, the use of masks), the actors playing Ubu lacked sufficient physical presence and vocal power to convey the full force of Jarry's monstrous creation. In the Vieux-Colombier performance in particular, far from stressing the potential violence and incongruities of the play, the director and actors seem to have conceived of its characters (a somewhat boozy Mère Ubu who addressed herself directly to the audience, and a Père Ubu wearing a pointed dunce's cap) in terms of circus clowns and of the action in terms largely of slapstick, a clear betrayal of the author's original intentions.

A number of other performances followed. But it was Jean Vilar's production of *Ubu* at the Théâtre National Populaire in March 1958 which really put Jarry and Ubu on the theatrical map, so to speak. The performance on the whole aroused great enthusiasm among the critics (though Vilar's liberties with Jarry's texts brought forth indignant protests from the latter's admirers in the Collège de 'Pataphysique) and proved to be a huge popular success, two short revivals of the play having to be given the following year and in 1960 to satisfy public demand. Fascinated above all by the figure of Ubu himself, in whom he saw an archetypal embodiment of 'cruelty', Vilar took very considerable liberties with Jarry's texts. His *Ubu* was a fusion of *Ubu Roi*, *Ubu enchaîné* and Jarry's own two-act abridgement for marionettes of the former, *Ubu sur la Butte*, reduced to a total of thirty-four scenes or tableaux (in the actual production that is, though the printed version published by the TNP contains forty-seven scenes). To stress the enormity of the character and to fill out the silhouette of Georges Wilson, playing Ubu, who already towered above the rest of the cast, he was equipped with an inflated life-jacket beneath a large, ballooning, smock-like garment decorated with an enormous *gidouille* or spiral, the brilliant pumpkin orange of his costume providing a striking contrast to the garish green stripes of Mère Ubu's dress. Wilson also adopted a consciously mechanical diction, as Jarry had recommended. The *palotins* were dressed in top hats and striped trousers. The stage was bare except for a bridge-like platform with steps either side used to create effects of height and (in the absence of real trap-doors) the impression of falling in the scene of the *trappe*, and various props and mobile elements of the set were brought on stage by the actors themselves as the need arose. These elements and props were suitably stylized and schematic, the latter including a wooden horse on wheels for Ubu and *chevaux-jupons* for the soldiers. The somewhat pop-art set and costumes designed by Jacques Lagrange, with their 'couleurs explosives', together with the clever and witty music of Maurice Jarre which, played by an orchestra resembling a military brass band, ran the gamut from the waltz and polonaise to the cha cha, drew forth much critical acclaim. Photographs of the performance and the comments of some critics suggest a somewhat clown-like performance on the part of the actors; nevertheless the majority of critics were full of praise for Wilson's acting and diction which they felt fully conveyed the stupidity and brutality of Ubu and above all the sheer presence of the character, and for the suitably harridan-like performance of Rosy Varte as Mère Ubu (though the actress in question was much too attractive for the role). Criticism must

be made too of a tendency in the production towards political
and social satire (though more particularly in those scenes drawn
from *Ubu enchaîné*): comments made by Vilar in an interview
with André Parinaud published in *Arts* of 12 March 1958
indicate that he conceived of the figure of Ubu in both plays in
terms of a criticism of the existing state of society, and
particularly of French society, rather than of a vision of
mankind itself. The fact remains however that Vilar, for the first
time since 1896, fully succeeded in conveying the presence and
the power of the figure of Ubu, and that this production was,
for the first time ever, a huge popular success, even if to some
extent authenticity was here sacrificed, rightly or wrongly, to
theatrical effectiveness.

Meanwhile, *Ubu Roi* was becoming known also in the
English-speaking world — somewhat belatedly, perhaps, when
we reflect that a first Italian performance was given in Rome in
1926 and a Czech performance in Prague in 1928. The English-
speaking world would ultimately however see a greater number
of performances — at least of amateur and semi-professional
ones — than the play's country of origin. The first stage performance appears to have been that given under the title *Ubu the
King* in August 1952 at the Cherry Lane Theater in New York,
by the Living Theater of Julian Beck and Judith Malina, in a
translation by the directors. Owing to the company's precarious
financial state the production was mounted on a shoe-string
budget — the total costs were less than thirty-five dollars —, the
sets being made of brown paper and the costumes of rags, and
the actors all performing without pay. In view of the
increasingly political involvement of the Living Theater at the
time and its espousal soon afterwards of a form of political
anarchism, it seems fair to assume that the interpretation given
to the play was one of political satire. The same year, and quite
independently — following a 'dramatic reading' of the play in
Barbara Wright's translation at the Institute of Contemporary
Arts in February 1952 —, the first English stage performance of
Ubu Roi was given in the same translation and under the same
director, William Jay, at the Irving Theatre, London, in
December 1952. In August 1963 the play was performed, under

the direction of Terry Lane and with Ian Trigger as Père Ubu, as part of the Edinburgh Festival, and continued to run for some time, with great success, at the Traverse Theatre Club in Edinburgh. The production which did most to establish the play in Britain however was that directed by Iain Cuthbertson at the Royal Court Theatre in London in July 1966. The play was translated and adapted by Cuthbertson, music (for two pianos) was composed by Frank Spedding, and Père and Mère Ubu were played by Max Wall and John Shepherd respectively. The most striking, and successful, feature of the production however was the set and costumes brilliantly designed by David Hockney. Ubu wore a large balloon-shaped garment (making him look like a huge egg) decorated with a spiral over striped pyjama-like trousers, with a bowler hat and later a crown on top of this. Mère Ubu wore a bell-shaped dress to which were attached large magenta plastic breasts which intermittently lit up from within (introducing a questionable sexual element into the portrayal of the character, though one rendered derisory by the role being played by a man). Bordure was dressed in a shabby long mac with large epaulettes and jackboots, and sported a thick moustache, heavy brows and hair parted in the middle and slicked back. King Wenceslas looked rather like an Indian Army colonel with parasol, droopy moustache, hat and monocle (later appropriated and worn by Ubu when he became king). And the soldiers and *palotins* were variously clad in T-shirts and trousers or pyjama-like garments, with sandwich-boards over the top. The dominant colours of the production, seen in both sets and costumes, were distinctly pop art in character — shocking pinks, greens (the stage was covered by a sheet of artificial grass such as is used by greengrocers), and the like. The actors entered the stage through a door in the middle. Bordure's prison was represented by a gigantic bird-cage. The windmill in the Ukraine of Act IV was a miniature one. Settings and scene changes were indicated throughout either by large painted signs on panels of the set lowered onto the stage — UBUS BACK ROOM (*sic*, the word 'BACK' changing when necessary to 'FRONT'), 'Royal Palace', 'CAVE', 'UBUS CLOSET' (a somewhat dubious touch, this), and the like — or by huge block letters arranged along the footlights by the *palotins* forming such indications as 'PARADE GROUND' and 'POLISH ARMY IN THE UKRAINE'. Other labels were written or painted on individual props — 'PHYNANCIAL HORSE', or (inscribed on the blade of a huge wooden sword given to Bougrelas by his ghost-ancestors) 'SWORD OF VENGENCE' [*sic*]. The setting for the final scene was represented by a sketch of a ship with the word 'SEA' written beneath it. And the Polish army was represented by three extras each carrying a sandwich-board marked respectively 'WHOLE', 'POLISH' and 'ARMY'.

Thus far, the production would seem on the whole to have accorded with Jarry's own intentions, combining a purely schematic representation, derisory in its extremes of non-realism, with a deliberate incoherence. But in other respects, the spirit of the performance diverged radically from those intentions. In place of the violence and verve of language and the systematic exploitation of incongruity in both language and gesture of the original production, the performance was conceived in terms of a cross between children's pantomime and music hall comedy. With the single exception of the word 'merdre' — retained in the original French since the Lord Chamberlain would not allow it to be translated into English! — the translation used tended to make the incongruous banal and the bizarre familiar. A number of songs, sung both as solo numbers and as choruses, were inserted into the performance. The greatest divergence of all however lay in the acting. Max Wall as Ubu brought to his performance the spirit of music hall comedy, inserting into his lines a string of well-worn jokes, instances of wordplay and ad-libbing, and playing the part of a jovial and self-conscious rogue. In fairness, it must be said that the production enjoyed considerable popular success (though, perhaps significantly, it failed to transfer to the West End after its eight-week run at the Royal Court); but, Hockney's sets apart, it was emphatically not conceived and executed in the spirit which Jarry intended.

The sixties saw also a number of interesting productions of *Ubu Roi* in media other than the live stage. In 1964 the Swedish director and puppeteer Michael Meschke first staged in Stockholm a version of the play, under the title *Kung Ubu*, which was subsequently given in the course of the next few years in well over a dozen countries throughout the world, earning international fame for its director and a string of prizes at international drama festivals. Meschke was originally inspired to conceive of his version by the artist Franciszka Themerson's line drawings illustrating Barbara Wright's English translation of the play, published by the Gaberbocchus Press run by the artist and her husband. The production was conceived in terms of a fusion between live actors, half human and half puppet-like figures (actors wearing three-dimensional body-masks), and flat two-dimensional cut-outs. Designed by Franciszka Themerson, it drew inspiration (according to Meschke in an article in *Théâtre et Université*, No.14, April 1968, pp.65-66) both from Artaud's call for a 'total' theatre and from the primitive popular toys which still survive in countries such as Poland and Mexico. Ubu was played by Allan Edwall, the only part wholly played by a live actor amidst a sea of marionette-like figures. Mère Ubu and Bordure were papier-mâché figures, the former looking like a caricatural fertility goddess with huge breasts and the latter having a rat-like appearance. All the other characters were represented by two-dimensional silhouettes, of varying sizes — different sized silhouettes of the same character being used at different moments throughout the performance to give an impression of depth and distance on the small stage — manipulated by operators dressed in white, half visible behind the silhouettes they controlled. The whole production was conceived in monochrome, sets, costumes and faces being entirely white, with the exception of a number of black masks. Music was provided by the Polish composer Krysztof Penderecki, and the dialogue was pre-recorded and played back in the course of the performance. The resulting hiatus between word and action, the music, the monochrome colour scheme, the combination of actors and puppetry, of semi-abstract shapes representing characters and mobile elements of the set midway between the live theatre and the animated drawing, all conspired to create an air of strangeness, fulfilling Meschke's aim which he described in the above-quoted article as being less to strive for comic or satirical effects than to 'faire ressortir dans l'œuvre une sorte d'étrangeté quasiment onirique et cruelle'.

A number of similar ideas informed the television adaptation of the play by Jean-Christophe Averty, first shown on French television in 1965 (and followed subsequently by television versions of *Ubu enchaîné* in 1971 and *Ubu cocu* in 1981). An enthusiastic devotee of Jarry, Averty already had the reputation of an *enfant terrible* of French television, and the first showing of his version, accompanied by a great deal of publicity, did more to make the play known than any performance since Vilar's in 1958. Eschewing all social and political interpretations (though seeing the play as an expression of the 'absurdity' of the world), Averty proudly boasted (in an interview with Jean-Louis Curtis in *Le Nouvel Observateur* of 22 September 1965) of his faithfulness to the text of the play and to Jarry's own dramatic conceptions, which he saw as anticipating the whole aesthetic of the modern theatre from Artaud to Vilar — stylization and abstraction, and effacement of the personality of the actor in order to bring to the fore the text itself. Like Meschke, he conceived of a juxtaposition of live actors and animated drawings. Ubu, played by Jean Bouise, and Mère Ubu, played by Rosy Varte (who had acted the role in Vilar's production), were the only two characters played by live actors, facing a series of cartoon-like figures on the screen. This juxtaposition was combined with a great deal of electronic manipulation, and in particular with the technique of photomontage which enabled Averty to juxtapose simultaneously upon the screen a number of different images, as also to vary the size of his characters, Ubu appearing in some scenes twice the size, and in others five or six times the size, of other characters. The sound was recorded separately and played back during filming, enabling Averty to obtain total control over the manipulation of his actors. The production, made for black-and-white television, featured a juxtaposition of those two colours, brilliantly illuminated white figures standing out against a wholly black background. The costumes (with the exception of that of Mère Ubu) were closely based on Jarry's own designs in his various sketches of the characters (these can be found in *3*, plates 43 to 68). Ubu wore a pear-shaped mask covering the whole of his head, with a moustache, his huge body being covered by a sheet-like garment decorated with an enormous *gidouille*, beneath which a pair of thin legs clad in over-short, candy-striped trousers was just visible. Mère Ubu wore a long dress, with a fur wrapped around her neck. Other characters were dressed very much in the manner of clowns, the *palotins* wearing a large, loose-fitting, hooded garment resembling a monk's cowl, the colour of which was a brilliant white with diagonal or horizontal black stripes or black dots. Certain of the characters (for example Bordure and the Tsar) adopted also special 'accents' as recommended by Jarry. Props were mostly cardboard cut-outs or simple drawings, whilst the *trappe* was represented by a large door marked thus. Scene changes, finally, were announced by a voice off-screen, and the whole was accompanied by the incidental music composed by Terrasse for the original performance in 1896.

Visually and auditively, the production provided a powerful experience — so powerful in fact as to constitute almost an act of aggression at times. A number of scenes were cleverly, and even brilliantly, performed, for example the murder of the king represented in animated drawings, and the scene of the *trappe* in which, as Ubu's victims rhythmically disappeared through the door into the 'disembraining room' to the accompaniment of loud screams, a huge pair of scissors was seen to cut off the top of the head of a series of paper cut-outs. Overall, it was in fact the cartoon-like aspect of the production which dominated. Critics complained — with some justification — that the production was above all an exercise in electronic gimmickry and technical virtuosity. Though the screen was much less 'busy' than in Averty's subsequent production of *Ubu enchaîné*, the production still tended to assault the senses of the viewer, with images (for example, Ubu's *gidouille*, amongst others) flashed intermittently on to the screen accompanied by at times a barrage of noise in the guise of sound-effects. Moreover, though the dialogue itself was on the whole scrupulously respected by Averty, it tended to be submerged much of the time beneath this barrage of brilliant images and noise. And with the exception of the *trappe* scene, the aggressiveness of the production techniques tended to take away from rather than add to the incipient violence of the play itself.

Nonetheless, the fame of *Ubu Roi* continued to spread, and the second half of the 1960s saw a series of performances in many countries throughout the world, many of them by young and/or university theatre companies, and many also offering interpretations of the play which corresponded to the growing politicization of student audiences during these years. Student performances were given in the United States and in Australia of satirical adaptations of *Ubu Roi* as part of a campaign of protest against the participation of those two countries in the Vietnam war. And an interesting East European view, with overtones of totalitarian dictatorship, was provided by a young Czech company from Prague, the Theatre on the Balustrade, which performed a highly acclaimed adaptation of *Ubu Roi* and *Ubu enchaîné* first in Liège and then in Paris in 1965, and subsequently in Berlin, Geneva, Berne and London. The set was described by one critic as stylized Brecht, and an imaginative use was made of props, many of them appropriately derisory (Ubu's *cheval à phynances*, for example, was a paraplegic's wheelchair).

The seventies also saw a continuing series of performances in both the live and puppet theatres, which were on the whole less politically orientated (apart from the customary, and almost inevitable, presentation of the play as a satire upon the 'bourgeoisie'!) but which frequently departed from Jarry's original conception in other ways. The most successful, if not most authentic, production of the early seventies was that staged by the Phénoménal Théâtre, directed by 'Guénolé Azerthiope', at the Théâtre de Plaisance in Paris in October 1970, and revived in March of the following year at the Théâtre Mouffetard. Amongst other inventions of the Phénoménal Théâtre, at the start of the performance Ubu was literally ejected on to the stage from a gigantic anus, giving to it from the outset a scatological colouring to which was added an abundance of sexual elements, particularly through the character of Mère Ubu (who was described by one critic as the living incarnation of a Mae West for sex-starved soldiers [*sic*]). The stage advanced into the middle of the auditorium, and the set comprised a mass of scaffolding and ladders which surrounded the audience on all sides, thus giving the actors a series of multiple acting areas enabling them to engulf the audience in the action. On this set the actors, indulging the current fashion for 'expression corporelle', gave themselves up with gusto to an orgy of acrobatic movements and exploits, to the detriment of the dialogue. Production techniques and forms of expression comprised elements of the fairground, circus, pop concert (with heavy percussion accompaniment) and wrestling match (with the stage constituting a metaphorical 'ring'), combined with 'psychedelic' projections of slides and flashing coloured lights, the whole carried out at a hectic, almost breathless, pace. The production embraced such an accumulation of styles and techniques, in fact, as to leave one wondering whether the aim was not to provide a spoof upon all the fashionable production methods of the time. But any such derisory intention was by and large lost in the general atmosphere of a huge collective 'fête' into which the young actors threw themselves gleefully and in which they invited the audience to join. As an example of uproarious farce or student review, the production was brilliantly successful; a performance of Jarry's play it emphatically was not.

A completely different conception of the play was provided by an 'operatic' version, known under the title of *Ubu à l'Opéra*, given at the eighteenth Avignon Festival in 1974 in collaboration with the Théâtre de l'Est Parisien. It was directed by Georges Wilson, who had played Ubu in Vilar's 1958 production and who here once again played the role, and the music was the work of the composer Antoine Duhamel. The production was born of Wilson's conviction (as quoted by Gilles de Van in *Travail Théâtral*, no.18-19, January-June 1975, pp.212-13) that the play's 'langage énorme, divers, poussé jusqu'au paroxysme de l'expression' cried out for musical accompaniment. Correspondingly, far from being merely incidental, the music was here fully integrated into the performance. The musicians, dressed in sinister black, were also actors, moving about the stage and participating in the action — one particularly effective scene being the death of Wenceslas, who found himself surrounded by the conspirators armed not with swords but with trumpets and saxophones. The action took place on a stage surrounded on three sides by a raised platform on which the musicians sat when not involved in the action (though some scenes were played on this platform as well), and which was in turn surrounded by a grubby wooden fence. Wilson's huge silhouette and costume similar to that used in the earlier production, together with a similar mechanical diction, sought to emphasize the enormity and stupidity of the character of Ubu. The dialogue was alternately spoken, shouted and sung in a variety of styles ranging from street songs to grand opera, and the music, in which brass and percussion instruments predominated, embraced almost every conceivable style from symphonic and jazz to popular dance hall and even barrages of sheer sound. Much of the time also the style of the music was adapted to the portrayal of character, ranging from the pompously 'regal' to the crapulous. The overall effect of this musical rendering was one of parody and derision, and to this extent the performance reinforced the essential characteristics of the text of the play. But most of the time the music became an object of enjoyment in its own right, tending to detract from, rather than reinforce, the violence and vigour of the play's language, and in the final analysis the production must be judged simply a fascinating, and enjoyable, experiment.

The next truly celebrated production was that of the Centre International de Créations Théâtrales directed by Peter Brook at the Théâtre des Bouffes du Nord in Paris in the autumn of 1977, then at the Young Vic in London the following year, and subsequently given in many countries around the world. Brook had long regarded *Ubu Roi* as the very model of his conception of 'théâtre brut', a theatre which in its extreme simplicity of material means calls upon all the resources of expression and invention contained in the actors themselves. In Paris and London, at least, *Ubu Roi* was performed together with *Ubu enchaîné*. The performance followed Jarry's text of *Ubu Roi* more or less faithfully until the scene of the bear in Act IV, from which point the shorter text of *Ubu sur la Butte* was substituted. A few minor cuts were made in the text of *Ubu enchaîné* which followed after an interval, though it was not, as in Vilar's production, made into a direct continuation of the preceding play. The theatre in which the performance took place in Paris (and subsequent performances in other cities were given in similarly sparse if not shabby surroundings) was notable for its bare, dirty walls, which Brook had refused to have repainted, and bare stage floor. The stage was on a level with the auditorium, with members of the audience finding themselves seated only a few feet from the actors. There were no wings, the actors entering the stage through side doors, a window, trap doors, or even from the midst of the audience, and both the stage area and auditorium remained illuminated throughout. Audience involvement was further increased by such incidents as Mère Ubu crawling under a spectator's seat during her search for the Polish royal treasure, or borrowing a pair of spectacles to read the letter received from Bordure. The relationship between actors and audience could not have been more different from that of 1896: in place of distance, alienation and aggression, the result was *rapprochement*, intimacy and even a sense of complicity.

The performance itself was given without the benefit of any of the usual supporting devices of the theatre: there was no set, no spotlighting, the actors for the most part wore no make-up, and props were reduced to an absolute minimum. The costumes too were not only banal and ordinary, but shabby and threadbare as well, looking rather as if they had come from a low-class jumble sale. Ubu wore an old baggy pair of brown woollen trousers with braces, knitted long-sleeved vest and slippers. His crown was a knitted woollen cap, and, following his seizure of the throne, a cushion was inserted under his vest to suggest a paunch. Mère Ubu was clad in a baggy black skirt and jumper, red tights, huge yellow slippers and dirty apron which she took off when she became queen, also replacing the slippers by an old down-at-heel pair of shoes. (She was also heavily and hideously made up, with straggly hair.) No attempt was made to suggest military uniforms, with the exception of Bordure's trenchcoat, jackboots and vaguely military cap, the *palotins* being clad in worn leather jackets and fur caps. The whole tended to create an impression of small-time back-street gangsterism, elements of a *Lumpen-*

proletariat whose kingdom lay more in a scrapyard than in a mythical and self-contradictory 'Poland'. The actors themselves however — an international and multiracial troupe of only six men and three women (the Tsar being played by a negress in a splendid leopard skin) — were physically as heterogeneous as possible. The height and powerful physique as well as deep, bellowing voice of Andreas Katsulas, splendidly truculent, vulgar, ferocious and menacing in the role of Ubu, contrasted with the fatness and dumpiness and piercing voice of Michèle Collison as Mère Ubu (in *Ubu Roi*), and with the small stature and skinniness of Bordure. The same heterogeneity was to be found in the contrasting accents which gave to the dialogue an air of strangeness, paradoxically throwing the words themselves into relief. The acting was deliberately exaggerated in the direction of broad farce, with a skilful and plentiful use of gesture, and an abundance of screams, shouts and loud musical accompaniment, with some extremely dramatic effects produced by Toshi Tsuchitori on the tympani and cymbals.

It was the nature and use of props which constituted the most striking feature of the production, however. Props were few and simple, looking in several cases as if they had come from a building (or even demolition) site — two cable reels, one huge, one slightly smaller; half a dozen or so bricks, some of them broken; a huge, grubby, white woollen rug with a long pile; an immensely long, padded, foam-rubber object about six inches in diameter, looking like a huge snake; and two trap-doors in the floor of the stage. None of these objects was merely decorative, all taking on a specific function and usually several functions. Many of them remained on stage throughout, the actors seeming to come upon them almost fortuitously and picking them up or otherwise making use of them as and when required. The bigger of the two cable reels, laid flat, served in turn as the table in the banquet scene, a platform or pedestal on which Wenceslas stood, and an altar on to which Mère Ubu climbed in the scene in which the conspirators swear an oath. Later, the smaller reel placed on top of the bigger one in this same position served to suggest the spiral staircase down which Bougrelas and Rosemonde flee. Upright, the larger cable reel served as Ubu's throne; in the scene in which Bougrelas's ancestors appear to him, it served to hide the bodies of the actors, their heads alone appearing all around its sides; and later, in Act III, it served as a gigantic bulldozer to crush the house of the peasants, who lay down between its wheels. The bricks, in Act I, represented the dishes served at the Ubus' banquet, and then the *côtes de rastron* thrown by Ubu at his fellow conspirators. Later, strewn over the floor where they had been left, they suggested the rocky terrain over which the Queen and Bougrelas seek to flee; then, assembled together, the fireplace in which the peasants light a fire; and, later again, one brick upon which Ubu stood represented the hill in the Ukraine on which he takes up battle position. The rug served as a royal mantle for Ubu when he becomes king, and as the bear in Act IV. And the long, padded rubber 'snake', wrapped around Ubu's body at the end of Act III, represented his armour as he goes off to war, unwinding itself across the stage in the chaos of the battle scenes. As for the trap-doors, one of these served for the scene of the execution of the Nobles, etc. (giving an unexpectedly literal meaning to Ubu's exclamation 'à la trappe!'). Another served as Bordure's prison — the actor playing Bordure having his hands tied to the under-side of the trap-door and being forced to bend double as Ubu slammed the door shut, providing a particularly vivid image of violence and brutality. And later one of the same trap-doors, closed, represented an enormous tombstone which Mère Ubu tried to raise in the scene in the crypt, and, slightly ajar, the mouth of the bear.

The very banality and inherent insignificance, or 'neutrality', of these artefacts allowed them to become multivalent objects, enabling the actors — and the audience — to project almost any meaning into them. At the same time, their intrinsic banality threw into relief and reinforced the sordid and brutal nature of the action of the play. And it was also, of course, a powerful source of comedy: the elements of surprise and incongruity which sprang from the huge gulf which existed between their physical reality and the meaning which the imagination of the spectator was made to place upon them produced hilarity and delight in the audience. So great was this gulf at times in fact —

for example when one brick upon which Ubu stood was made to signify a hill — that the resulting humour was one of total absurdity.

There can be no doubt that this was one of the most wonderfully imaginative productions of *Ubu Roi* ever staged. It was also one which by and large — unlike that of Vilar in 1958, whose chief interest lay in the figure of Ubu himself — respected the text of Jarry, which Brook saw as a necessary vehicle for the projection of that figure *and* a brilliantly comic work in its own right. The very success of Brook's production, however, throws into relief many of the questions previously raised concerning the staging of the play, and in particular its staging in a theatrical and social context now far removed from that which Jarry himself knew. How much of its success was due to the imagination of Brook and the disciplined skill of his actors (not to say the brilliance of certain production 'gags'), rather than to the play itself? To what extent do the conceptions and intentions of Brook and Jarry converge or coincide? And is it *possible* to perform *Ubu Roi* today in the way in which Jarry himself conceived of its performance almost ninety years ago?

To begin with, Brook's and Jarry's conceptions of the function and importance of the actor are, on the face of it, diametrically opposed. For Jarry, the actor must become a mere puppet, a wholly regulated and almost mechanical part of a fully integrated production which laid emphasis also on set, costumes and music. For Brook, the very absence of a set and the sparseness of props had the primary function of emphasizing the skill and imaginative possibilities of the *acting*. The opposition between the two men may, however, be more apparent than real, if we assume that Jarry's attitude towards actors has to be understood in a context in which actors tended all to be superb individualists who made of a performance a tribute to their own ego, and that he might well have modified that view once the actor had humbly accepted the need to become a disciplined member of a *team*, or even simply one element in a wholly integrated production.

More fundamental, perhaps, is the apparent opposition implied in Brook's definition of his conception of 'théâtre direct' (in an interview with Jean-Claude Carrière on the French television channel FR3 in 1977) as 'le théâtre qui passe directement à celui qui le reçoit' (a transmission effected by means not only of verbal communication — the dialogue of the play — but also of the whole 'langage gestuel' of the actors). To conceive of *Ubu Roi* in these terms is implicitly to amputate the play of all capacity to shock, to 'aggress' and thereby deliberately to alienate an audience. It is true that Brook's production succeeded in conveying more powerfully than most the inherent violence and verbal truculence of the play — what he himself described in the same interview as 'cette espèce d'énergie brutale qui se dégage des pages [de l'œuvre]'. But this violence was conveyed *to*, not directed *at*, the audience. It is arguable however that today *Ubu Roi* has lost its ability to shock or even, through familiarity, to surprise, and that it is necessary as a result to lay aside such concerns and to emphasize other aspects of the work. And Brook and others would doubtless even go so far as to maintain, rightly or wrongly, that if it is indeed impossible to alienate a modern audience then it is perhaps better to involve it.

Moreover, the fact remains also that this aggression was only one of Jarry's original aims, and one which he himself implicitly modified when he added as a conclusion to the third edition of *Ubu Roi* in 1900 the *Chanson du Décervelage*. Alongside the intention to shock and to outrage a part of his audience was also the aim to entertain and to delight through the creation of a form of humour based on deliberate incoherence and incongruity, not to say 'absurdity'. And in this respect, both playwright and director are united, even though the incongruity and absurdity in Brook's case are modified by a greater element of knockabout comedy and farce.

Lastly, the theatre of both Brook and Jarry is one which makes no pretence whatsoever at 'realism' but resolutely espouses a conscious and avowed use of *convention*. Both seek to call into play (though in slightly differing ways) the creative imagination of the spectator in whose mind alone 'reality' is created. And both seek thus to provide the spectator with a semi-abstract framework into which the audience can project its *own* specific content and meaning, in which it can see its *own* vision of Ubu.

Finally a different set of questions was raised by the most recent major production of *Ubu Roi*, that of Antoine Vitez in May and June 1985 at the Théâtre National de Chaillot, the scene of Vilar's triumph in 1958. Vitez had announced in advance his intention of making of the play a super-satire of the contemporary French bourgeoisie, portraying Ubu as the archetype of the 'jeune cadre dynamique' [*sic*]. Correspondingly, the set represented a very chic, ultra-modern living/dining-room set in the fashionable 16th *arrondissement* of Paris, with a large circular dining table laid for a dinner party, chairs, settee, stereo and telephone. Mère Ubu (played by Dominique Valadié) was dressed in an elegant, long, gold lamé dress and high heels, Père Ubu (Jean-Yves Chatelais) sported a smart blazer and tie with hair neatly slicked back, and the other characters wore party dresses or formal dark suits. The dominant colour of the set was a brilliant white, with table, chairs, walls and even the floor of the huge stage all being of the same colour. The same motifs recurred throughout the performance — the dining-table, food and drink, empty bottles and crockery — providing a source of unity on this level at least. Despite Vitez's announcement, however, the element of satire was secondary to, and undermined almost from the beginning by, the director's choosing to see the play first and foremost in terms of an all-embracing schoolboy parody, with the actors behaving more and more like a bunch of uncouth and unruly schoolboys on the rampage. As he explained his conception in the programme notes, 'C'est bien au lycée que la lecture attentive d'Alfred Jarry nous ramène. Chaque jour, au cours des répétitions du drame..., la liturgie de l'enseignement secondaire se dévoile un peu plus'. The keynote of the production was therefore one of systematic parody and derision in every conceivable form, including a parody of previous productions of the play. The same costumes and set were retained throughout (with the exception of the backdrop which later revealed a vista of the Eiffel Tower and the Palais de Chaillot where the performance was taking place), the beautifully immaculate white set becoming progressively bespattered with purée, excrement, mud and blood and littered with broken crockery and glassware. There was a clever use of props, many of them suitably derisory — for example, the massacre of Wenceslas and his two sons was recounted to the Queen over the telephone, Ubu carried a microphone about with him in Act III to interview the Nobles, and his musings in his sleep in Act V were broadcast to the audience through loudspeakers, whilst Bougrelas's sword of vengeance was an egg-ladle, and Ubu's battle steed was a serving trolley. Acting techniques included acting against the script and acting out of character (the role of Ubu being systematically underplayed, whilst those of other characters were frequently overplayed or deliberately 'hammed up'), a clever use of mime in certain scenes, the singing of lines (Ubu's long soliloquy in Act IV, for example, was sung by him at the piano), and a frequent use of song-and-dance routines (particularly on the part of Bordure, played by a rather 'butch' looking actress in a frilly black party dress who danced with both Ubu and the Tsar) to the accompaniment of heavily rhythmic, often discordant music, amounting to a parody of the American variety show. There were also a number of ingenious production gags, and the performance contained a vast amount of stage 'business' (including scenes of excreting, farting and copulating on stage), which resulted in an exceptionally long and drawn out performance which lasted considerably over two hours.

The production undoubtedly displayed a great deal of ingenuity, and the standard of the acting was superb. Many of Vitez's inventions raised a laugh from the audience and applause at the end was moderately warm (though critical reaction was mixed and the *jarrystes* present at the performance almost without exception loathed it!). To what extent, however, did it reflect the author's own wishes? In its systematic exploitation of parody and derision, the performance was no doubt faithful to the spirit of Jarry's play. But the question remains, derision of what? The accumulation of production gags and inventions, many of them bearing little or no relationship to the text itself, far from creating an overall unity of conception produced instead an impression of fragmentation and disunity. In *Ubu Roi*, whilst aiming to entertain, Jarry had sought also to provide a savagely comic portrait of the grotesqueness and stupidity of mankind itself; in Vitez's production, despite the director's denial that his approach reduced the work merely to the level of 'une plaisanterie sans conséquence' and his insistence that the performances still managed to evoke in microcosm the hideous reality of the exercise of power, I for one remained unconvinced.

In conclusion to this survey of performances of *Ubu Roi*, a number of points emerge. The first is the extraordinary and continuing variety of different approaches to the play displayed by producers and directors. In part this is a consequence simply of the wilfulness of certain directors, or of a permanent search for novelty at all costs. But to some extent also it betrays a continuing ignorance in many quarters of the true intentions of its author, both in philosophical or moral and in aesthetic terms. *Ubu Roi* is still all too often seen in terms of social and political satire; and, despite the widespread acceptance in our own age of a form of humour based on the systematic exploitation of incongruity and contradiction (not to say 'absurdity'), many performances continue to be conceived primarily in terms of mere slapstick, or knockabout comedy, or verbal jokes and innuendoes.

A second point which emerges is the obvious appeal of the play to the young (as also, I am tempted to add, to the young in spirit), and to popular and intellectual audiences alike. Two penetrating remarks made by Pierre-Aimé Touchard some forty years ago (in *Gavroche*, 29 March 1945) à propos of an amateur performance before a popular audience in the French provinces are still relevant today:

> *Ubu Roi* est le type même de l'œuvre dramatique authentiquement populaire, c'est-à-dire susceptible de rassembler les suffrages aussi bien des intellectuels que d'un public peu cultivé. Elle possède, poussées à un degré extrême, les trois qualités fondamentales de toute grande œuvre comique: 1) l'invention verbale; 2) le mouvement; 3) un symbolisme satirique juste et aisément traduisible.

And:

> *Ubu Roi* est une des ces œuvres qui portent en elles tant de

jeunesse que les troupes d'amateurs sont souvent les seules
à pouvoir en conserver l'élan.

A third and final point is a direct consequence of this last.
However important youthful enthusiasm and a capacity for
innocent enjoyment may be, more than these alone is needed if
the full potential of Jarry's play is to be realized and if the
performance is to go beyond the level of mere farce and
knockabout comedy. Discipline, careful organization and
extreme precision of timing and tone constitute equally essential
elements of any performance that aims to convey the full impact
of the play's humour and of the power of its monstrous hero.
But with those qualities, a performance of *Ubu Roi* has the
capacity to provide a powerful and memorable theatrical
experience.

6. Conclusion: Jarry and the Modern Theatre

Time and again in histories of the modern 'avant-garde' theatre or the so-called 'theatre of the absurd' Jarry is cited as a precursor. How accurate is this judgement, and what are the true relations between Jarry and his successors in the modern theatre, particularly in the French theatre since 1945? I am not concerned here with trying to trace 'influences', which are notoriously difficult to establish (though it would be possible to find an avowed influence of Jarry on a long line of playwrights and men of the theatre from Apollinaire through Vitrac, Artaud and Ghelderode to Ionesco and Arrabal), nor to sketch, however briefly, a history of developments in the theatre from Jarry onwards (though here again it would be possible to show a continuous evolution from Jarry through the Dadaist and Surrealist theatre and Artaud to the work of post-war playwrights such as Vian, Adamov, Beckett and Ionesco).[16] My aim is simply to point out a number of significant parallels between the ideas and work of Jarry and the theatre of more recent times.

It is perhaps best to begin, in order to clear the ground, by stating what those links are not. The term 'theatre of the absurd' was first given currency by Martin Esslin, who argues that the dominant characteristic of the post-war theatre in Europe is its communication of an awareness of living in a metaphysical void, the result of a loss of earlier metaphysical values and concepts which gave a sense of purpose to existence. He quotes Ionesco on this concept of 'the absurd':

[16] The relationship between Jarry and the Dadaist and Surrealist theatre has been studied in detail by Henri Béhar in *Etude sur le théâtre dada et surréaliste*, Paris: Gallimard, 1967. Béhar has also examined the links between Jarry and Roger Vitrac (co-founder, with Antonin Artaud in 1926-27, of the Théâtre Alfred Jarry) in his *Roger Vitrac, un réprouvé du surréalisme*, Paris: Nizet, 1966. See also the long and valuable chapter in *11*, devoted to an examination of the links between Jarry and his successors in the modern French theatre, to which I am indebted for a number of details contained in this final chapter.

> Est absurde ce qui n'a pas de but: et ce but final ne peut se
> trouver qu'au-delà de l'histoire... coupé de ses racines
> religieuses ou métaphysiques, l'homme est perdu, toute sa
> démarche devient insensée, inutile, étouffante. (*19*, p.232)

Subsequently, the label 'theatre of the absurd' has been applied
willy-nilly by Esslin and others to a wide range of modern playwrights, including, by association, Jarry. Whatever its value in
characterizing the theatre of Beckett or, to a somewhat lesser
degree, that of Ionesco, however, it is hasty and ill-advised in
relation to the work of Jarry as also of most other modern playwrights to whom it is sometimes applied, tending to blur
important differences as much as or even more than it highlights
similarities. In Jarry's own case, his aim in *Ubu Roi* is first and
foremost the projection of a *moral* vision, through a figure
whose prototype already embodied 'tout le grotesque qui fût au
monde' (p.341); and although that vision inevitably has certain
metaphysical implications, nowhere in his theatre is there
evidence of a direct concern to communicate that sense of the
'absurdity' of existence itself which one finds in the plays of, for
example, Beckett or Ionesco.

No, the parallels between Jarry and later playwrights are to be
found less in the field of philosophical vision than in that of
their conception of the theatre. *Ubu Roi* stands at a turning
point in the evolution of the modern theatre. In an age in which
the traditional distinction between poetry and prose was
breaking down (with the invention of the *vers libre*) and painting
was taking its first steps in the direction of abstraction, it was
only natural that the theatre should attempt to follow a similar
path of self-examination and re-definition. Jarry himself was in
the forefront of such developments (all the more so as he was
himself fully abreast of similar movements in the fields of poetry
and painting and had close personal links with many of those
most responsible for them): his work in the theatre set out to
revolutionize that genre in respect of its language, of its forms of
expression, and of the underlying purpose and function of the
theatre itself.

The starting point of Jarry and of a host of subsequent

playwrights is an effort to break once and for all with the principles and traditions of the realist and naturalist theatre, with its
attempt to create on the stage an illusion of the 'real' world (or
what its practitioners took to be the 'real' world) outside the
theatre. The first significant parallel lies therefore in the efforts
to create, in opposition to such conventions, a theatre based on
the principles of deliberate stylization and simplification, and on
the adoption of purely 'schematic' modes of representation.
Jarry's endeavours in this domain were echoed to some extent by
those of the Symbolist theatre, and by the ideas of theatrical
reformers and visionaries of his own time and of the early years
of this century such as Adophe Appia and Edward Gordon
Craig. Indeed, the very title of Craig's collection of essays
published in 1911, *On the Art of the Theatre*, deliberately
stressed the 'art' — or artifice — of the theatre, in opposition to
the attempted 'imitation of reality' almost universally accepted
at the time, implicitly recalling Jarry's own view which saw 'art'
and 'nature' as diametrically opposed. Today, of course, an
element of simplification and stylization is an accepted part of
production methods in the modern theatre even in relation to
plays written in a traditional realist or naturalist mode. But the
real revolution in our time has been the widespread total
abandonment of this mode by a string of major playwrights,
who see the true force of the theatre as lying in the adoption of
conventions diametrically opposed to those of realism. Such a
view is most forcefully expressed by Ionesco, the whole of whose
work illustrates this new, non-realist aesthetic:

> Si donc la valeur du théâtre était dans le grossissement des
> effets, il fallait les grossir davantage encore, les souligner,
> les accentuer au maximum. Pousser le théâtre au-delà de
> cette zone intermédiaire qui n'est ni théâtre, ni littérature,
> c'est le restituer à son cadre propre, à ses limites naturelles.
>
> (*19*, pp.12-13)

The second feature of the theatre of his time rejected by Jarry
in which he can again be seen as a precursor is its essentially
narrative and psychological function. The theatre, he argues, is

not the proper place for 'telling a story' or for the portrayal and analysis of psychological conflicts, which belong more properly to the novel. Nor is it the place for dealing with social issues or problems. Whether or not there is a necessary relationship between a theatre which, thematically, is orientated towards the expression of social issues and problems and the realist mode of expression, the fact remains that historically the two have been closely linked. The inevitable corollary is the desire to create a theatre which will be concerned with a portrayal of 'situations' and 'types', or more exactly archetypes, and with the expression of the universal and the eternal rather than with purely historically limited social issues and themes. Jarry thus implicitly looks forward to the call of Artaud for a 'metaphysical' theatre which will be concerned with the portrayal of aspects of an unchanging 'human condition', a conception fully realized in the work of playwrights such as Beckett, Ionesco or (in his early plays) Adamov. He also implicitly anticipates Artaud's call for a theatre of 'myth', in the sense of a creation of universal and archetypal images: 'Créer des Mythes voilà le véritable objet du théâtre, traduire la vie sous son aspect universel, immense, et extraire de cette vie des images où nous aimerions à nous retrouver' (7, pp.139-40). What after all is Ubu but a 'myth' in this sense, an archetypal image of mankind as seen by Jarry? And what, similarly, is a play such as *En attendant Godot* but a modern 'myth', the expression in the form of a powerful image of its author's view of the essential absurdity of the human situation?

The creation of such a theatre has profound implications for the portrayal of character on the stage; and here a further parallel can be found. To reject the portrayal of psychological conflicts is also to reject psychological complexity, and implicitly to advocate a deliberately simplified and schematic presentation of human character — a presentation which, at its most extreme point of development, finds its outward expression in the use of masks or the portrayal of human beings in terms of mere puppets. And this too is not only a central feature of the work of Jarry but has been a significant (though certainly not universal) trend in the theatre of the twentieth century, most strikingly in evidence in the work of Ionesco, particularly in his early one-act plays or in a highly stylized later work such as *Macbett*.[17] With this simplification of character goes also on occasions an abandonment of psychological coherence and motivation, which in turn can have a profound effect upon the plot and action of the play. The unpredictability of Ubu's behaviour — his sudden and unexpected changes from resolution to cowardice or his apparently gratuitous acts of cruelty — indicates in such instances an absence of coherence and logical motivation which looks forward in embryonic form to the topsy-turvy world of, for example, those same early plays of Ionesco. A similar absence of logic in the relationship between events can be found in certain of the plays of Arrabal (for example *L'Architecte et l'Empereur d'Assyrie*), whilst discontinuity is a fundamental feature of the theatre of Beckett.

Such a portrayal of character points also to the sources of inspiration of the above playwrights and others, which indicate a further parallel between Jarry and his successors. In all intended revolutions, whether political or artistic, men tend to turn back, in order to create something radically different from the present or from that which immediately preceded it, to a more distant past for inspiration. Jarry's attempt to revitalize the theatre of his time by a return to the 'simpler' and more 'naïve' art of the mime and the puppet theatre has been echoed by many since. Directors and theoreticians of an earlier generation such as Craig and Gaston Baty have exalted the expressive possibilities of marionettes, and playwrights such as Ghelderode, Ionesco and Arrabal have spoken of their childhood delight in the *guignol* which has been a source of inspiration in their own work. A different source of inspiration, that of the circus, can also be seen in the plays of Arrabal; whilst Beckett's enduring fascination with the situations and techniques of the circus and music-hall has helped to shape a long line of Beckettian figures from Vladimir, Estragon, Pozzo and Lucky in *Godot* to Winnie

[17] There is an interesting three-way comparison to be made between Shakespeare's *Macbeth*, Ionesco's *Macbett* and Jarry's *Ubu Roi*, which would reveal the last as a kind of distorting mirror through the medium of which Shakespeare's play is parodied by Ionesco.

in *Happy Days*. In the work of Jarry as of these and other playwrights, moreover, the figure of the puppet or of the clown provides more than simply a source of inspiration but takes on a
functional significance also, providing an image of man himself
and his situation in the world and forming an essential part of
the playwright's own vision.

'Simplification', in both characterization and themes, does
not however as Jarry understood it mean mere simplicity, but
rather a condensation or synthesis of complexity, as a key
passage in the 'Linteau' to his first book, *Les Minutes de sable
mémorial*, reveals: 'La simplicité n'a pas besoin d'être simple,
mais du complexe resserré et synthétisé' (*2*, p.172). Thus the
figure of Ubu is simple only in the sense that he synthesizes and
implicitly embodies a multiplicity of different potential
meanings. Whence Jarry's invitation to the audience at the
première of *Ubu Roi* to place its own interpretation upon the
play — 'C'est pourquoi vous serez libres de voir en M. Ubu les
multiples allusions que vous voudrez'[18] —, a statement which
looks forward to the concepts much beloved of modern criticism
of the 'polysemy' and 'openness' of the work of art. The latter is
defined by the Italian critic Umberto Eco in his *L'Opera aperta*
in the terms: 'l'œuvre d'art est un *message* fondamentalement
ambigu, une pluralité de signifiés qui coexistent en un seul
signifiant' (quoted in *11*, p.224). Such a concept is central to
Jarry's whole literary aesthetic (clearly outlined in the above-
mentioned 'Linteau'), and underlies his reflections in his
'Réponses à un questionnaire sur l'art dramatique' on the possi-
bility of an 'abstract' theatre, in which the play would constitute
no more than a kind of abstract framework into which the
members of the audience would be invited to project their own
meaning — thereby participating actively, he maintains, through
the exercise of the imagination, in the process of creation itself.

---

[18] There is something of a contradiction in Jarry's views here. On the one hand,
he vigorously protested against contemporary interpretations of *Ubu Roi* in
terms of political and social satire; but on the other, the concept implicitly suggested here of the 'openness' of the work would seem to legitimize these,
together with all other interpretations. Was he playing a game somewhat akin to
that of Beckett, who pretends to allow of all possible interpretations of his plays?
To claim to accept all interpretations as equally valid is in reality to accept none,
since mutually contradictory views cancel each other out.

It is this urge towards abstraction which explains the nature of the setting of *Ubu Roi* — its Nowhere/Everywhere achieved by a cancelling out of mutually contradictory elements —, and to which there corresponds a similar imprecision in the work of such playwrights as Ionesco (island in the midst of a lake, anonymous but archetypal provincial town, mythical kingdom), Vian (block of flats in an unnamed town), Arrabal (car scrapyard, mythical desert island) or Beckett (deserted country road, enclosed room on the edge of the sea, hillock in the midst of a barren landscape). No modern playwright better realizes this conception of the theatre, in fact, than Beckett who, deliberately refusing to acknowledge any one interpretation of his plays as correct to the exclusion of others, provides us with a series of abstract or semi-abstract images of existence, a framework into which *we* are invited to project our own meaning.

A sixth parallel, of a quite different nature, can be found in the deliberate provocation of Jarry's flouting of the linguistic and theatrical conventions of his time, in his calculated attack upon both the moral and aesthetic susceptibilities of his audience. The original production of *Ubu Roi* provides in this respect an outstanding example of theatrical aggression which has been followed by many directors and playwrights since, from Artaud to Peter Brook and Charles Marowitz, and from the Dadaist and Surrealist theatre to certain of the works of Weingarten (the first performance of whose *Akara* in 1948 was likened by critics to the opening night of *Ubu Roi*), Genet, Ionesco (whose first play was provocatively subtitled 'anti-pièce'), Vautier and Arrabal.

Where, however, it was the linguistic and moral aspect of that aggressiveness which had most impact on Jarry's contemporaries, from our point of view today its most significant feature was its artistic subversiveness, Jarry's creation of forms of deliberate incoherence and logical contradiction which can be seen implicitly to call into question the very nature and existence of the work of art itself. There is in fact present in Jarry a dual impulse, a desire to create radically new artistic forms which exists alongside and simultaneously with a secret wish to subvert all forms of art from within. The tension resulting from these two conflicting impulses was in fact never resolved in his work, and can be seen in his theatre, in much of his poetry and in such novels as *Messaline* and *Le Surmâle* where the apparent reality of the narrative is secretly undermined from within.

This subversive intention is not however restricted to Jarry (though he was among the first of modern writers to manifest it), but is shared with a number of modern playwrights and novelists and is in fact characteristic of the intensely self-conscious and introspective age in which we live. It expresses itself at times, as in Jarry, in the inclusion within a work of deliberately contradictory details, and at times also, in the theatre, through the presence *within the play itself* of elements of dialogue or action whose function is to remind us that what we are watching is a 'fiction', a 'play' in the primary sense of the word. In the image borrowed from the marionette theatre used by Ionesco, the playwright sets out to 'non pas cacher les ficelles mais les rendre plus visibles encore, délibérément évidentes' (*19*, p.13). Thus Genet, causing the character of Irma at the end of *Le Balcon* to instruct the audience on the route for leaving the theatre, or Ionesco, causing Marguerite in *Le Roi se meurt* to remind the king — and the audience — that he will die in exactly one and a half hours, 'à la fin du spectacle', or displaying to the audience a huge picture of himself in *Macbett*, create an additional dimension of awareness in the minds of the audience which causes it mentally to step back and to realize the true nature of the spectacle with which it is being presented. No modern playwright so fully exemplifies this conception of what has been called 'the self-conscious stage' as Beckett, in whose plays the affirmation of the essentially 'fictional' and 'theatrical' nature of what we are watching is a recurrent feature. To take just two examples, if on one level Beckett's characters in *Godot* are tramps waiting for some external event to transform their lives, and on another are archetypal embodiments of mankind caught in a metaphysical impasse, on a third they are *actors* self-consciously engaging in verbal and gestural games and 'playing' to an audience whose presence they implicitly acknowledge; whilst the very term *jouer* — meaning both to play, and to act in the theatre — occurs several times in

the dialogue of *Fin de partie*, beginning with the first line spoken
by Hamm (whose name suggests, among other things, a 'ham'
actor): 'A moi... De jouer'. All of Beckett's characters in fact
are to a greater or lesser degree self-conscious actors, knowingly
playing out a pre-determined 'role'. His theatre constitutes the
ultimate manifestation of a process of which Jarry and the first
performance of *Ubu Roi* stand at the fountainhead.

Jarry can also be seen as a precursor in his creation and
exploitation of a form of humour to which contemporary
audiences totally failed to respond (or responded with bewilderment and hostility) but which has become widespread in our own
time, a humour based on the deliberate exploitation of incongruity or of outright logical contradiction in both action and
word — a form of humour which can legitimately be described
as 'absurd' humour. The clash of conflicting elements in the set
for *Ubu Roi* in 1896 no less than the clock of Ionesco's *La
Cantatrice chauve* which strikes successively seven, three,
nought, five and two times in the course of the first scene, or
Ubu's statement that 'Je vais allumer du feu en attendant qu'il
apporte du bois', Ionesco's demonstration in the same play that
when a doorbell rings it means that 'des fois il y a quelqu'un,
d'autres fois il n'y a personne' (Scene 8) and Clov's statement in
Fin de partie that 'Si je ne tue pas ce rat il va mourir', all provide
examples of a form of humour which deliberately flies in the
face of the laws of logic or causality. Not only moreover is this
form of humour widely accepted and exploited in our own age,
but it seems to have a particular appeal to those of an intellectual
bent — perhaps justifying Jarry's claim that 'l'absurde exerce
l'esprit' through the provision of a much-needed liberation from
the constraints of logic and the processes of reasoning. It is also,
finally, a decidedly subversive and destructive form of humour,
sweeping all before it in a total derision of rational values, anticipating and responding to Artaud's call for a rediscovery of 'le
pouvoir de dissociation anarchique du rire' (7, p.51) which,
along with a true sense of the tragic, Western civilization had
lost.

Lastly, Jarry in *Ubu Roi* brought to the theatre — or more
exactly restored to it — the spirit of childhood which had been a

part of the mediaeval theatre but which had been proscribed by the dominant rationalism of the intervening centuries. The vision which presided at the creation of *Ubu Roi*, with its crude exaggeration, its violence, its frequent absence of logical relationships and coherent motivation for action, is that of a child's conception of the world; and the character of Ubu himself is nothing more than that of an overgrown child, displaying a primeval innocence, but one which is no less terrifying and brutal for all that. It was a vision which Jarry alone among his school fellows had the insight and the artistic sense to preserve, but which looks forward to playwrights such as Ionesco, Vian and Arrabal, whose work at times either focuses on similarly childlike figures or portrays in other ways an equally terrifying or disturbing innocence. Even more important than this vision itself, however, is the *spirit* which informs Jarry's play, and which expresses itself in a spontaneous and innocent love of nonsense, of wordplay and linguistic distortion, and of sheer absurdity. To laugh at such 'absurd' forms of humour requires a willingness to suspend the normal habits of rational thinking characteristic of the adult mind, and to enter once again, at least momentarily, into the spirit of childhood. And insofar as we are able to do this today, we are all heirs of Jarry.

In all of these ways, then, Jarry can be seen as a precursor of the modern theatre, or at least of one major current in it. The conception of the theatre which he illustrates is not of course the only conception prevalent even today. Nevertheless it is a sufficiently important and widespread one to make of Jarry, as a result of the extensive parallels outlined above, a major figure in the emergence of modern culture, and to make of *Ubu Roi* an archetype for our own time.

Bibliography

A. WORKS BY JARRY AND EDITIONS OF WORKS REFERRED TO:

1. *Ubu*, ed. Noël Arnaud & Henri Bordillon, Paris: Gallimard (Coll. Folio), 1978. Contains *Ubu Roi*, *Ubu cocu*, *Ubu enchaîné* and *Ubu sur la Butte* together with the complete text of Jarry's writings on the theatre and letters to Lugné-Poe.

1a. *Ubu Roi*, ed. Henri Béhar, Paris: Larousse, 1985.

1b. *Ubu Roi*, ed. Jean-Claude Dinguirard & Paul Gayot, Paris: Bordas, 1986.

2. *Œuvres complètes*, ed. Michel Arrivé, Paris: Gallimard (Bibliothèque de la Pléiade), I, 1972. Contains, in addition to the above plays, *Ontogénie*, *Les Minutes de sable mémorial*, *César-Antechrist*, Jarry's *Almanachs du Père Ubu*, *Gestes et opinions du docteur Faustroll, pataphysicien*, *Les Jours et les Nuits*, *L'Amour en visites*, *L'Amour absolu*, other shorter early works and a selection of correspondence. At the time of going to press, volume II is still not yet published.

3. *Peintures, gravures et dessins d'Alfred Jarry*, ed. Michel Arrivé, Paris: Le Cercle du Livre & Collège de 'Pataphysique, 1968.

4. *Messaline, roman de l'ancienne Rome*, Paris: Eric Losfeld, 1977.

5. *Le Surmâle, roman moderne*, Paris: Eric Losfeld, 1977.

B. PRINCIPAL BOOKS AND ARTICLES DEALING WITH JARRY'S THEATRE, AND PRINCIPAL OTHER WORKS CITED:

6. Arrivé, Michel: *Les Langages de Jarry. Essai de sémiotique littéraire*, Paris: Klincksieck, 1972.

7. Artaud, Antonin: *Le Théâtre et son double*, in *Œuvres complètes*, IV, Paris: Gallimard, 1964.

8. Bablet, Denis: *Esthétique générale du décor de théâtre de 1870 à 1914*, Paris: Editions du CNRS, 1965.

9. Beaumont, Keith: *Alfred Jarry: a critical and biographical study*, Leicester University Press, 1984.

10. Bedner, Jules: 'Eléments guignolesques dans le théâtre d'Alfred Jarry', *Revue d'Histoire Littéraire de la France*, 73 (1973), 69-84.

11. Béhar, Henri: *Jarry dramaturge*, Paris: Nizet, 1980. The most detailed and best study of Jarry's theatre as a whole.

12. Bergson, Henri: *Le Rire: essai sur la signification du comique*, Paris: Alcan, 23e éd., 1924.

13. Chassé, Charles: *Sous le masque d'Alfred Jarry(?). Les Sources d'Ubu-Roi* [*sic*], Paris: H. Floury, 1921. Later incorporated into *Dans les coulisses de la gloire: d'Ubu-Roi au douanier Rousseau*, Paris: Editions de la Nouvelle Revue Critique, 1947.

14. Cooper, Judith: *Ubu Roi: an analytical study*, Tulane Studies in Romance Languages and Literature, 6, 1974.

15. Damerval, Gérard: *Ubu Roi: la bombe comique de 1896*, Paris: Nizet, 1984.

16. Eruli, Brunella: *Jarry: i mostri dell'immagine*, Pisa: Pacini, 1982.

17. *L'Etoile-Absinthe*, Bulletin de la Société des Amis d'Alfred Jarry, 1979 onwards. Contains various useful articles, though mainly on other aspects of Jarry's work.

18. Grimm, Jürgen: *Das avantgardische Theater Frankreichs, 1895-1930*, Munich: Beck, 1982.

19. Ionesco, Eugène: *Notes et contre-notes*, Paris: Gallimard, 1962.

20. Lugné-Poe, Aurélien: *La Parade*, II: *Acrobaties*, Paris: Gallimard, 1931.

21. Robillot, Henri: 'La Presse d'*Ubu Roi*', *Cahiers du Collège de 'Pataphysique*, 3-4 (1950), 73-88.

22. Sainmont, Jean-Hugues [pseud.]: 'Ubu ou la création d'un mythe', *Cahiers du Collège de 'Pataphysique*, 3-4 (1950), 57-69.

23. ——: 'Rennes visions d'histoire', *Cahiers du Collège de 'Pataphysique*, 20 (1954), 27-36.

24. Schumacher, Claude: *Alfred Jarry and Guillaume Apollinaire*, Basingstoke: Macmillan Education (Macmillan Modern Dramatists), 1985.

25. Shattuck, Roger & Watson Taylor, Simon, eds: *Selected Works of Alfred Jarry*, London: Methuen, 1965. Contains *inter alia* translations of most of Jarry's writings on the theatre.

26. Stillman, Linda: *Alfred Jarry*, Boston: Twayne (Twayne's World Authors Series), 1984.

27. Symons, Arthur: *Studies in Seven Arts*, London: Constable, 1906.

CRITICAL GUIDES TO FRENCH TEXTS

edited by
Roger Little, Wolfgang van Emden, David Williams